NOTICE

This play is copyright, and may not be performed without
a licence for which application must be made in advance to:

PROGRESS HOUSE (PUBLICATIONS) LTD.,
36 HOME FARM ROAD,
DUBLIN 9,
IRELAND.

The fee for the presentation of this play by amateurs must
accompany any application for a licence. Professional terms by
arrangement. A current scale of fees is available from the
publishers as above.

This edited two-act version of Sive was first presented in the Abbey Theatre, Dublin on Thursday, 13th of June, 1985.

NANNA GLAVIN	Marie Kean
MENA GLAVIN	Catherine Byrne
SIVE	Maeve Germaine
THOMASHEEN SEAN RUA	Donall Farmer
MIKE GLAVIN	John Olohan
LIAM SCUAB	Sean Campion
SEAN DOTA	Micheal O'Briain
PATS BOCOCK	Eamonn Kelly
CARTHALAWN	Macdara O'Fatharta

Director	Ben Barnes
Designer	Monica Frawley
Lighting Design	Tony Wakefield
Music	Roger Doyle
Poster Design	Brendan Foreman

CHARACTERS:

NANNA GLAVIN — An old woman (mother of Mike Glavin, and grandmother of Sive)

MENA GLAVIN — Mike Glavin's wife

SIVE — The illegitimate granddaughter of Nanna Glavin

THOMASHEEN SEAN RUA — A matchmaker

MIKE GLAVIN — The man of the house (husband of Mena Glavin, son of Nanna Glavin)

LIAM SCUAB — A carpenter, Sive's sweetheart

SEAN DOTA — An old farmer, suitor for the hand of Sive

PATS BOCOCK — A travelling tinker-man

CARTHALAWN — His musical son

The action of the play takes place in the kitchen of Glavin's small farm-house in a remote mountainy part of Southern Ireland.

Song from "SIVE"

Oh! Mike Glav - in you're the man; You was
al - ways in the van; With a dacent house to
old man and gor — soon, May white
snuff be at your wake, Baker's bread and curran'y
cake, And plinty on your table late and
soon —

Transcribed by Oonagh Connon

ACT ONE

SCENE 1

The kitchen is poorly furnished, with an open hearth on its left wall. A door leads to a bedroom at the left side of the hearth. On the wall facing the audience there is a small window, and a door leads to the yard at the front of the house.

A large dresser, filled with ware in its upper half, stands between the door and the window. The lower part has doors. A third door is in the right wall of the kitchen with a small working-table at one side. Overhead a mirror hangs. Under the table are two buckets and a basin. A 20-gallon creamery tank stands between the door and the table with a half-filled sack of meal and a half-sack of flour.

A larger table stands in the middle of the floor. There are six sugan chairs; two beside the table; two by the fire; the others on either side of the dresser.

In the hearth a black skillet hangs from a crane and a large black kettle rests in a corner. An enamel bucket of drinking water is on the table.

The time is the recent past, a late evening of a bitter March day.

An old woman bent forward with age dressed in black sits near the fire surreptitiously smoking a clay pipe, she is Nanna Glavin, mother of the man of the house. She holds the tongs, idly gathering the fire; with the other hand she conveys the pipe continuously between lap and mouth.

When she hears the door latch lifting the tongs falls in her haste to conceal the pipe. A great quantity of red petticoat, and long boots tied up to her shins, are revealed when she lifts her skirt to hide the pipe.

Her skirts are hardly in place again, when another woman enters. The newcomer is strong, well-proportioned, hard-featured, in her early forties: her hair raven-black tied sharply in a bun gives the front of her head the appearance of being in want of hair, or being in a coif. She is Mena, wife of the man of the house.

Mena:	There's a smell of smoke!
Nanna:	(*Crossly*), 'Tis the way you left the fire when you went out.
Mena:	Not turf smoke, oul' woman, tobacco smoke!
Nanna:	Tobacco smoke how are you? (*Nanna seizes the tongs and belabours the fire*).
Mena:	In the name of all that's dead and gone, wouldn't you take out your pipe and smoke it, not be humpin' yourself there, like a cat stealin' milk?
	(*Mena bends to take one of the buckets from under the working table. She puts it between her boots and pours water from the full enamel drinking bucket into it. She replaces the enamel drinking bucket*).
Nanna:	(*Irritably*) such clatter!
	(*Mena, scoops several fistfuls of meal from the bag into the bucket*).
Mena:	No clatter unless 'tis your own. Wouldn't you give over talkin', and take out your pipe (*wearily*) and not be hiding it when we walk in and out of the kitchen?
Nanna:	Am I to be scolded, night and day in my own house? Ah! 'twas a sore day to me my son took you for a wife. What a happy home we had before you came into it! Fitter for you be having three of four children put from you at this day of your life.

2

Mena: I had my fortune; 'twasn't for the want of a roof over my head that I came here. I could have done better if I bided my time. *(Lifts bucket and turns to door)*.

Nanna: We all know what you could do, girl, and the stock you came from ... and the cabin you came out of! *(Laughs a little forcefully)*. Where ye used to drink yeer tay out of jampots for the want of cups. Oh, indeed, you needn't tell me about yourself. A nice bargain you were!

Mena: You have nothing else to do but talk. Saying your prayers you should be, at this hour of your days, instead of cackling with your bad tongue ... Where was your poor amadawn of a son before I came here? Pulling bogdeal out of the ground with a jinnet, going around like a half-fool with his head hanging by him ... you give me the puke with your grandeur. Take out your dirty doodeen of a pipe and close your gob on it, woman. I have something else to do besides arguing with you.

(Mena lifts the latch to go out. As she does so, the door opens and a pretty young girl enters. She is aged about 18 and wears a grey tweed coat, a little too small for her. a flimsy scarf covers her head. She carried a satchel, filled with books, in her hand. Her name is Sive. When she enters, Mena closes the door and looks at Sive piercingly Sive puts her satchel on the large table, aware of Mena's eyes upon her back).

Sive: I was held up after leaving the village. The front wheel of the bicycle went flat on me, and to crown my misfortune didn't I get a slow puncture in the other wheel. 'Tis the tyres that are worn. I was lucky to meet the master on the road. He gave me a lift as far as the end of the bohareen. *(She unties her scarf)*.

Mena: Schoolmasters and motorcars. And I suppose you expect me to have a hot dinner ready for you any minute of the day you decide to come home.

Sive: Oh, no! ... we had a cookery class at the Convent today, all the girls got dinner there. We had fricassee with dartois for dessert. It was lovely!

Mena: Saints preserve us! Out working with a farmer you should be, my girl, instead of getting your head filled with high notions. You'll come to no good either, like the one that went before you!

(Mena lifts the bucket and goes out. Sive takes off her coat and holds it over her arm. Underneath she wears a brown schoolgirl uniform with white collar attached).

Sive: What does she mean, Gran. The one that went before. Who was she referring to?

Nanna: There's no meaning to that woman's blather! *(Lifts her skirt and puts her pipe into her mouth)*. Quenched! ... bad skewer to her gone out!

Sive: She meant my mother, didn't she, Gran?

Nanna: Your mother, the Lord mercy on her, was my daughter. She wouldn't dare to draw down her name ... it was only poison prattle, child; wind and steam. Isn't she always at it. 'Tis the disease in her system. If she didn't let it out of her mouth, 'twould break out in boils and sores all over her. You're worse, to take notice of her!

Sive: *(Lays her coat over books on table and sits on its edge facing grandmother)*. Gran, all I know about my mother is that she died when I was a baby. Any time I've asked questions about her you've all put me off and told me you didn't know or that you had forgotten ... and my father ... you say he was drowned, no more. What I want to know is what sort of a man was he. Was he funny; was he handsome? Why wasn't he here by my mother's side when I was born or what kind of a father was he that he left her to suffer alone?

Nanna: He was in England. He couldn't be here, could he, when he was there. He was drowned, the poor boy, a few days after you were born. Coalmining he was, when the waters rushed in and trapped him. *(Reflective sadness)*. Away over in England.

3

Sive: What was I like when I was born? Am I like my father now or like my mother?

Nanna: Questions! Questions! Nothing but questions! You were a fine common lump of a baby! I remember well the night you were born. The doctor came in his new motor car from the village. I remember well to see the two roundy balls of fire coming up the bohareen. The old people swore it was the devil but sure it was only the two headlamps of the car shining in the darkness. *(Draws on her pipe fruitlessly)*. Devil take the tobacco they're making these days!

Sive: Tell me more about my mother, Gran! She was pretty, wasn't she?

Nanna: *(With regret)*. She was pretty, too pretty. *(Shakes her head)*. She was handsome, God rest her. *(The kitchen door opens noiselessly and Mena stands framed in it without speaking. She is unnoticed by Sive and Nanna. She carries the empty bucket)*.

Sive: Go on, Gran! Tell me more! You must have so many stories about my mother when she was young.

Nanna: What more is there to tell?

(She lifts her head, looks past Sive to the door and tries to indicate to Sive that Mena is at the door. She hides her pipe hurriedly. Suddenly Sive understands and looks behind her in bewilderment. She comes to her feet quickly).

Mena: 'Tis a wonder you took your backside from the table where people do be eating. Is that what you're learning at the Convent?

(Abashed, Sive takes her coat and books from the table. Mena puts bucket under the working-table).

Mena: Your uncle and I work ourselves to the marrow of the bones to give you schooling and the minute I turn my back you're cohackling with that oul' boody woman in the corner. *(To Nanna)*. Some day that pipe will take fire where you have it hidden and you'll go off in a big black ball of smoke and ashes.

Nanna: *(Slowly)*. If I do, 'tis my prayer that the wind will blow me in your direction and I'll have the satisfaction of taking you with me. Aha, you'd burn well, for you're as dry as the hobs of hell inside of you. Every woman of your age in the parish has a child of her own and nothing to show by you.

Mena: Hold your tongue, old woman. How dare you cast your curses inside in my own house. It isn't my fault I have no child. *(Looks meaningly at Sive)*. Enough that had children in their time. I have every right to this house. I paid dear for my share.

Nanna: I was here before you.

Mena: Ah, but you won't be here after me!

Nanna: That is the will of God, woman; not your will.

Mena: *(To Sive - loudly)*. Take your books and get to your room. Is it for ornament you think we are keeping you? I'm sure the nuns would like to hear of your conduct.

(Sive hurries to the door at right of kitchen. She casts a quick look behind her towards her grandmother).

Mena: What nonsense have you been filling the girl's head with? She'll be as cracked as the crows if she listens to you; wasting her time when she should be at her studies. When I was her age in my father's house I worked from dawn till dark to put aside my fortune.

Nanna: You should have stayed in your father's house ... Your father *(derisively)* a half starved bocock of a beggar with the Spanish blood galloping through his veins like litters of hungry greyhounds.

Mena: *(Threateningly)*. Old woman, be careful with your free tongue! 'Twill wither up inside your head. You mind your corner of the house and I'll mind mine. You have great gumption for a woman with nothing.

Nanna: *(Takes the tongs in her hand)*. The calves are bawling for their milk.

(Nanna leans on tongs and rises with its support, then lets it fall noisily. She goes after Sive into room at right of kitchen, ignoring Mena's looks. She walks slightly humped. When she has left, Mena goes to fire and rearranges it with tongs. She goes to the dresser, opens one of the doors and extracts an apron which she ties about her waist. Going to fire she lifts the skillet from the crane and replaces it with the kettle. She uses the hem of her apron to handle both utensils. She goes to the working table and withdraws the second bucket, and listens at door of room where Nanna and Sive are. While she is thus occupied there is a faint knock on the kitchen door. She turns instantly, then looks into the mirror and pats her hair hurriedly. She advances a step towards the door).

Mena: Come in, let you!

(The door opens slowly and a man peers cautiously about the kitchen. he wears a disfigured felt hat upon unruly hair and looks as if he had not shaved for a week. He is shifty-looking, ever on his guard. He is fortyish. He snakes the hat from his head and thrusts it into his coat pocket, when his eyes rest on Mena. He is Thomasheen Sean Rua, a matchmaker).

Thomasheen: Are you along, bean-a''tighe? *(He looks around again)*. Or is there someone with you? *(Very confidential. His voice has a rasp-like quality with the calculated slow drawl typical of the south west).*

Mena: I'm as much alone as ever I'll be. Come in, will you. You look like a scarecrow there in the doorway.

Thomasheen: God help us, amn't I like a scarecrow always, matchmaking and making love between people I spend my days and no thanks for it.

(He enters and goes to the fire. He turns his back to it and lifts the tail of his overcoat to savour the heat. Mena closes the door and stands at the table).

Mena: *(Pause)*. What is all the secrecy about, Thomasheen. You look like you have something to tell.

Thomasheen: There's a frightful sting in the air this evening. There is the sign of rain to the west, God between us and all harm ... Is the man of the house within or without?

Mena: He is gone to the village with a rail of bonhams.

Thomasheen: Ah! Great money in bonhams these days. They'll save the country yet, I may tell you. There's more money in two bonhams than there is in the making of a match, God help us.

Mena: If you think I can spend the evening listening to bualam ski, you can go the road for yourself. What is it that brought you? Out with it!

Thomasheen: There is no one with an ear cocked? *(He looks about suspiciously)*.

Mena: The old woman and the girl are below in the room but you can shout to the heavens for all the attention they'll pay to you. If it is after matchmaking you came, boy, you have put pains on your feet for nothing.

Thomasheen: Thomasheen Sean Rua never blisters his feet without cause. There is some one who have a great wish for the young lady, this one they call Sive. 'This how he have seen her bicycling to the Convent in the village. *(Shakes his head solemnly)*. He is greatly taken by her. He have the mouth half-open when he do be talking about her. 'Tis the sign of love, woman!

Mena: Are you by any chance taking leave of your senses, buachall! What is she but a school-girl ... and illegitimate, to crown all! She has no knowledge of her father and the mother is dead with shame out of her the most of 20 years.

Thomasheen: Illegitimate! There is fierce bond to the word and great length to it. Whatever she is, she has the makings of a woman.

Mena: Rameish! You have great talk.

Thomasheen: Ah! but she have one thing we will never see any more of, God help us ... she have the youth and the figure and the face to stand over it. 'Tis the youth, blast you, that the old men do be after. 'This the heat *(pronounced 'Hait')* before death that plays upon them.

Mena: Old men! What are you saying about old men! *(Her voice rises in volume).*

Thomasheen: Hush, woman! ... You'll tell the parish! ... What matter if the girl be what she is, if she had a black face and the hooves of a pony ... the man I mention is taken with her. He will buy, well and lose all to have her. He have the wish for the girl.

Mena: *(Suddenly shrewd).* Who has the wish for her?

Thomasheen: No quibble between the pair of us, Mena. Sean Dota is the man.

Mena: Sean Dota!

Thomasheen: Hould your hoult, woman! Take heed of what I say. He have the grass of 20 cows. He have fat cattle besides and he have the holding of money.

Mena: He's as old as the hills!

Thomasheen: But he's a hardy thief with the mad mind for women breaking out through him like the tetter with no cure for it. What matter if he is as grey as the goat. There is many a young man after a year of marriage losing his heart for lovemaking. This man have the temper. He would swim the Shannon for a young wife. He would spoil her, I tell you. There is good reward for all concerned in it. Don't be hasty, to be sorry later.

Mena: You are like all the matchmakers: you will make a rose out of a nettle to make a bargain.

Thomasheen: He have the house to himself - nothing to be done by her only walk in and take charge. There is a servant boy and a servant girl. There is spring water in the back yard, and a pony and trap for going to the village.

Mena: Sean Dota! *(Reflectively).* The girl hasn't a brown penny to her name.

Thomasheen: No fortune is wanted, I tell you. 'Tis how he will give money to have her.

Mena: He will give money! The devil isn't your master for the red lies. That's the first I ever heard of a farmer giving money instead of looking for it. What will we hear next.

Thomasheen: *(Extends both hands).* 'Tis the ageing blood in the thief ... Ah! It's an old story, girl. The old man and the young woman. When they get the stroke this way there is no holding them. There is the longing he have been storing away these years past.

Mena: *(Pause).* And you say he would give money for her?

Thomasheen: That my right hand might fall off if he won't! 200 sovereigns for you if the girl will consent.

Mena: *(Suspiciously).* And what is for you? It isn't out of the goodness of yer heart you are playing your hand.

Thomasheen: There will be a hundred pounds for me.

Mena: 200 pounds ... she'll scorn him. She has high notions.

Thomasheen: Aye! It won't come aisy. *(He advances a little way towards her and lowers his head to peer at her before going on).* High notions, or no high notions, you're the one that can do it. Isn't she a bye-child? ... Tell her you will bell-rag her through the parish if she goes against you. Tell her you will hunt the oul' woman into the County Home. Think of the 200 sovereigns dancing in the heel of your fist. Think of the thick bundle of notes in the shelter of your buzzom. It isn't every day of the week 200 pound will come your way.

Mena: The girl is flighty like a colt. Threats might only make her worse.

Thomasheen: Be silky then, be canny! Take her gentle. Let it out to her by degrees. Draw down the man's name first by way of no harm. You could mention the fine place he have. You could say he would be for the grave within a year or two and that she might pick and choose from the bucks of the parish when he's gone.

Mena: She'll cock her nose at him! ... 'Tis all love and romancing these days with little thought for comfort or security. *(Pause).* 20 cows and money to burn! *(Reflectively).* She'll do no better for all her airs and graces. Look at the match I made ... four cows on the side of a mountain and a few acres of bog.

Thomasheen: Remember there's 200 sovereigns staring you in the face if you will be doing your duty by Sean Dota.

Mena: I will consider *(Pause)* ... The old woman would be against it. She has the charming of the girl in her hands. They are as thick as thieves, the pair of them.

Thomasheen: Gently will do it, step by step. Show her the chances she will have, the fine clothes and the envy of the neighbours. The house is like a Bishop's palace, paper on every wall, and a pot, by all accounts, under every bed. She will have the life of a queen.

Mena: *(Thoughtfully).* And I would be rid of her. And 200 pounds into the bargain. I would!

Thomasheen: And you would be rid of the old woman, too.

Mena: *(Alert).* By what way?

Thomasheen: We will make it a part of the match that she will go with Sive.

Mena: I would be clear and clane of the pair of 'em!

Thomasheen: 'Tis a chance that will not pass the way again.

Mena: Would he take the oul' woman, do you think?

Thomasheen: Do you know the man you have? How many years is Sean Dota in the world? How many years have he spent searchin' the country for a young woman?

Mena: Will he take the oul' woman or won't he?

Thomasheen: He will have anything, I tell you, if he will get Sive.

Mena: It would be a great day to the house. Years I have suffered with the two of them, always full of hate for me. I would give my right hand to have that oul' hag out of my way.

Thomasheen: Ah, you have no life, God help us, with the worry of them.

Mena: Why should that young rip be sent to a Convent every day instead of being out earning with a farmer. Good money going on her because her fool of a mother begged on the deathbed to educate her.

Thomasheen: 'Tis a mortal sin!

Mena: 'Tis worse! 'Tis against nature. She'll have her eyes opened.

Thomasheen: I often wonder how you put up with it at all.

Mena: I won't suffer long more.

Thomasheen: *(Rubs his hands gleefully).* I knew my woman from the start. You must go to the core of the apple to come by the seed.

7

Mena: Himself? ... What will he say?

Thomasheen: Aren't ye in the one bed sleeping. Ye will have yeer own talk. You will come around him aisy. You weren't born a fool, Mena. I know what it is like in the long long hours of the night. I know what it is to be alone in a house when the only word you will hear is a sigh, the sigh of the fire in the heart dying, with no human words to warm you. I am a single man. *(Deadly serious).* I know what a man have to do who have no woman to lie with him. He have to drink hard, or he have to walk under the black sky when every eye is closed in sleep. Now, with you, there is a difference. You have the man. You have the companion. Sleeping or waking you have your husband in the flesh and bone and there is the one will between ye. You will see that he is of the same word as yourself. Be said by me, leanav *(ingratiatingly)*, take the rough with the smooth ... But have your way. Keep the picture of 200 sovereigns in your mind.

Mena: *(Calculatingly).* Aisy said!

Thomasheen: *(Touches her hand).* There is the money to think of. *(He withdraws his hand immediately, and going to window, looks out).* No sign of rail and car. *(He looks at Mena).* Listen, woman, I will call tonight with my man, just as if we were passing the way by chance. Pretend nothing!

(Suddenly the room door at stage right opens noisily and Nanna comes in).

Mena: What is all the fuastar for? Is it how the hinges of the door are worn? Or must you make noise wherever you go with the bitterness that's in you?

(Nanna does not answer but goes to the dresser and takes a cup. Slowly, deliberately, she goes to where the milk-tank is. Looking over at Thomasheen she lifts its cover and dips cup inside it. She withdraws cup, having filled it, and replaces the cover).

Mena: The top of the tank for her ladyship!

Nanna: Would you see the girl hungry? *(To Thomasheen).* I know you, Thomasheen Sean Rua. 'Tis no good that brings you here this day of the week. The mean snap is in you and all that went before you. You'd sell your soul to the devil for a drink of buttermilk.

(Thomasheen advances, fists clenched, but holds his tongue. He glares at the old woman, who turns and goes into the room again).

Thomasheen: Ah-ha! hag! consumptive oul' hag Seed an' breed of consumptive oul' hags. *(His voice grows high-pitched. To Mena).* Marry the young one and be rid of that oul' devil!

Mena: Huist! ... I hear the axle of a car on the road ... 'tis himself coming from the village. *(Becomes flurried).* Clear away with you ... tonight, mind! I will come around himself in my own time. He has a great love for the few pounds.

Thomasheen: *(Goes to door, and peeps out. Then turns to Mena).* I'll have the old man here by night fall.

(Thomasheen opens the door, looks to left and right and disappears. Mena takes three plates and cups from dresser and puts them on table. Goes to the tankard of milk and fills a jug by immersing it. She dries the jug with her apron and fills the three cups with milk. From lower part of dresser she takes three large spoons, and puts them on the table. Between each action she looks out of window. When the door opens, Mena does not turn to look at the new arrival. He is her husband, Mike Glavin. Under his arm he carries a sack partly filled with hay which he puts under the working table. He carries a thonged whip attached to an ash-plant. He is a quiet man, determined of movement. His voice will be studious and calculated).

Mena: You're back!

Mike: Aye!

(He goes immediately to table and sits on the chair nearest to it. The man of the

8

	house is home! The woman must become alert in her own way. Mike searches his right-hand pocket. He withdraws a few currency notes and some silver. He places them on the nearest of the three plates. He smooths the notes awkwardly with his fingers, folds them, and begins to count the silver with inexperienced hands. With a single gesture he returns the money to his pocket).
Mena:	How much today?
Mike:	What have you in the skillet?
Mena:	How much money did you make?
Mike:	*(He does not move his head).* 16 pounds, 10 shillings. I gave a crown luck.
Mena:	How much for the single bonham?
Mike:	'Twas together I sold them.
Mena:	A great day's hire! Will it last?
Mike:	'Twill last! *(Pause).* It makes a great change from beggin' and pinchin' with our craws often only half-filled. Ah! you should see the shopkeepers in the village today. Like singing birds they were, calling out our names when we passed with our loads. *(Noisily).* I mind a day not so long past when they had us by the throats. They wouldn't give a half-sack of flour without money down. The boot is on the other foot now with turf the way it is and pigs and calves fetching the high price. It does the heart good to see the shop keepers scrapin' and bowin'. Money is the best friend a man ever had. *(He takes off his coat and hangs it from a crook behind kitchen door).*
Mena:	We will mind whatever penny we make.
Mike:	You may say we'll mind it! *(He puts his hand into pocket of coat and withdraws the money, which he hands to Mena).* What have you to ate, woman? *(Mena does not answer his question immediately but wraps the notes about the silver coins and transfers the lot to the pocket of her skirt).*
Mena:	The spuds are boiled. I will make a muller of onion dip. Sit down a tamaill. There is something I have to say to you.
Mike:	*(Puzzled).* Yes ... what?
Mena:	Sit here! *(She indicates the chair which he has vacated. He sits on it looking at her expectantly).* It is about Sive.
Mike:	Sive!
	(Mena sits at the left of the table and places her hands on it).
Mike:	What is it about Sive?
Mena:	How will I start to tell you? *(Pauses).* There is an account of a match for Sive.
Mike:	*(Screws up his face in wonder).* For Sive? ... a match? Are you going simple, woman? There is no sense or meaning to you. She's only a child ... still going to school ...
Mena:	*(Crossly).* She's old enough! The grass of 20 cows, a farm free of debt; money rotting there
Mike:	She has no fortune. What farmer of that size would take her without money?
Mena:	He'll be glad to have her, money or no. Think of 20 milch cows and security for the rest of her days.
Mike:	She is different. She has book-learning. She will turn a deaf ear to matchmaking. *(He shakes his head).* I'm her uncle. When my sister died I gave my word that I would stand by her. The girl is too young. She has no father. I have responsibility.

Mena: Was it your fault, I ask you, that your sister died? Was it your fault that she gave birth to the girl or was too free with men? *(In anger).*

Mike: *(Warning).* Aisy, a-girl! *(Deadly note).* Aisy! She was young in the ways of the world. She paid dearly for her folly, God help us. She dressed a thorny bed for herself. Will you look how old the world is and how the youth do be so foolish in it.

Mena: Now listen to me! *(Insistent).* The child was born in want of wedlock. That much is well known from one end of the parish to the other. What is before her when she can put no name on her father? What better can she do when the chance of comfort is calling to her. Will you take stock of yourself, man! there is a fine farm waiting her with servants to tend her so that her hands will be soft and clean when the women of the parish will be up to their eyes in cowdung and puddle. What better can she do? Who will take her with the slur and the doubt hanging over her?

Mike: *(Shakes head).* I don't know, woman! I don't know what is best.

Mena: You know as well as I do that what I say is best for the girl.

Mike: Maybe so! ... Maybe so! *(Puzzled).* But who is the man who would marry without a fortune and he having that fine bane of cows?

(Mena is silent for a moment, looking at him from beneath lowered brows).

Mike: Well?

Mena: *(Pauses, then looks directly at him).* Sean Dota from the foot of the hill.

Mike: *(Open-mouthed, repeating the words slowly).* Sean Dota!

Mena: *(Hurriedly).* A respectable man with a good bit put away by him. And it will mean that we will be rid of your mother, too. Sive will take her for company. Wouldn't it be wonderful?

(Mike suddenly jumps to his feet).

Mike: Never! ... if the sun, moon and stars rained down out of the heavens and split the ground under my feet ... never! 'Twill never come to pass while I have the pulse of life in me! *(Changes his tone from anger to entreaty).* What devil has got into you that you should think of such a thing? Even when I was a boy Sean Dota was a man. The grave he should be thinking of. What young girl would look a second time at him, a worn, exhausted little lurgadawn of a man.

Mena: You are hasty to condemn! Will you sit down and hear me out. We will have the house here to ourselves with the oul' woman gone as well. *(Suggested note of love).*

Mike: *(Loud voiced).* Never! Not even if the Son of God walked the roads of the earth again! She will not darken the door of his house.

Mena: Will you sit down, man. You will take flight! Sit here!

Mike: Sit for what ...? Sit, is it, to give ear to the greatest nonsense within the four walls of the world! You can't be in your right mind.

Mena: There is the gift of 200 pounds for us if there is a marriage. *(Long pause).* Think the start it would give us. How many times would you bend your back to make it? Long enough we were scraping: you said it yourself. Consider it, will you. It is what we wanted always. Sive will be well off and we will be rid of your mother and her taunting.

Mike: No! No! A million thousand times no! It would sleep with me for the rest of my days. It would be like tossing the white flower of the canavaun on to the manure heap. It is against the grain of my bones woman. Will you think of it? Think of what it is! Sive and that oul'corpse of a man, Sean Dota!

Mena: *(Soothing motherly tone).* Will you sit down and be said by me.

Mike: I will not sit! ... I am going out!

Mena:	*(Repeating his words, her voice filled with sarcasm).* You are going out! *(Changes to a tone of boldness).* Well, if you are going out, I am going with you.
Mike:	*(Lifts his right hand).* There is a finish, girl, to our talk. Leave me to myself. I have a wish to go by myself. Let me be. *(He looks at her, filled with doubt).*
Mena:	*(Pause).* Go away! Go away with you. Go away, man of straw.
Mike:	*(Harshly, loud-voiced).* I am no man of straw. Will you not leave me be with myself.
	(Suddenly in a violent fit of temper, he knocks the chair upon which he has been sitting and goes out, slamming the door. Mena rises and follows him through the door, leaving it open after her, still calling his name. When both are gone, the old woman comes from the room and looks out after them. She goes to the fire, produces her pipe and lights it. She has only just sat down when a young man enters; aged about nineteen, he is good-looking and manly, his voice cultured and refined. His entrance is somewhat hurried. He is Liam Scuab. He carries a few short planks and a bag of tools).
Liam:	I never saw such commotion. First I saw Thomasheen Sean Rua, the matchmaker, sneaking away over the mountain from this house. Next I saw Mike hurrying out of here as if the devil were after him and, last of all I saw Mena running after Mike, calling his name. What's going on at all? Have they all gone mad? *(He puts his tools and planks on table).*
Nanna:	You'd better not be caught here. There will be trouble. Mike Glavin has no liking for you or any of yours, Liam.
Liam:	I wouldn't have called only I was sure there was nobody here but Sive and yourself. I was up the road making a door for Seamus Donal. Where is she?
Nanna:	*(Archly).* Where is who?
Liam:	*(Smiling).* Come on, you oul' schemer! You know who I mean.
Nanna:	*(Rises and calls to Sive's room).* Sive, Liam Scuab is here. *(Sive enters).*
Sive:	Liam! ... what brought you?
Liam:	I was passing by; just going the road on business.
Sive:	*(Suddenly alarmed, breaks away).* You'll be caught! *(To Nanna).* Where is Mena ... my Uncle Mike ... He'll have a fit, Liam!
Nanna:	Be careful, let ye, and keep a watch. If 'tis a thing ye're caught together there'll be no more peace in this house. *(Exit Nanna).*
Liam:	*(Taking Sive's hand).* Will you be able to steal out tonight?
Sive:	If I can, but if I don't come at the time, don't wait.
Liam:	I'll wait till the crack of dawn, anyway.
Sive:	Be careful Uncle Mike hates you.
Liam:	What harm if he does. He might as well hate me as anybody.
Sive:	*(Pause).* I wonder what Mena and Uncle Mike are doing in the bog?
Liam:	Who knows? I saw Thomasheen Sean Rua, the matchmaker, leaving here too, a while back.
Sive:	Thomasheen Sean Rua! What did that devil want?
Liam:	Nothing good, I'll warrant. Imagine making a marriage between two people who never saw each other before.
Sive:	Horrible?

Liam:	They say it is necessary in country places.
Sive:	It's horrible, Liam. Would you marry somebody you never saw before?
Liam:	I would marry nobody but you, Sive, I love you. How would I marry anybody but you!
Sive:	*(Pause)*. You'd better go. If we're found together ...!
Liam:	*(Takes his possessions from table)*. I'll wait tonight until you come.
Sive:	If I don't come when I say, go home. It's cold and lonely waiting in the dark.
Liam:	It's cold and lonely, too, at home.
Sive:	Look, if I don't come I'll meet you on the road from school tomorrow.
Liam:	Try to come if you can.
	(Mike enters angrily).
Mike:	What's this? *(louder)*. What's this, I say. What are you doing in my house, Liam Scuab? How dare one of your breed cross my door in!
Sive:	*(Timorously)*. He was passing by!
Mike:	He was passing by! He was! He was, like a rat when he saw the nest empty. He came stealing and sneaking when we were outside.
Sive:	He was not sneaking and he was not stealing.
Mike:	Go to your room ... Go on! *(Exit Sive)*.
Liam:	*(Calmly)*. No blame to Sive.
Mike:	I know your breed, Scuab, and what you are and I know what you're looking for.
Liam:	There's no need to sound so dirty about it.
Mike:	I know what you're after, Scuab.
Liam:	*(Calmly)*. I make no denial about it. I'm after Sive.
Mike:	I know well what you're after.
Liam:	You know one thing and I know another. I say I am after Sive and nothing more than that. I love her.
Mike:	Like your snake of a cousin loved her mother moryeah and fooled her likewise. Like your snake of a cousin that tricked her mother with the promise of marriage and left her a child with no name.
Liam:	*(Calmly)*. I know who Sive's father is. It is no fault of mine.
Mike:	It was the fault of your cousin and ye're the one breed.
Liam:	You know as well as I do that he would have married her. You know he went across to England to make a home for her but he was drowned. He never knew she was with child when he left.
Mike:	You bring your tale well, don't you? Quick words and book-readin' like all belonging to you. Like your bloody cousin.
Liam:	He died, didn't he? What more do you want?
Mike:	I want for you to leave here and keep away from Sive. I want that you should never set eyes on her again or you will pay as dear as your cousin paid, maybe.
Liam:	You will not command the lives and happiness of two people who love each other.
Mike:	*(In a rage)*. I will not command ... the cheek ... go on, get out of here, you upstart ... Go on! ... Go!

Liam:	(Pause) (Exiting). We shall see.
Mike:	(Roaring). Go on, you tathaire, go on ...
	(Exit Liam waving a hand behind his back in disgust. When he has gone Mike fumes in the kitchen. After a moment he goes to the door and calls Mena).
Mike:	Mena! ... Mena! ...
	(Mike exits calling her name).

CURTAIN.

SCENE TWO

The time: Night; A paraffin lamp burns on a shelf over the fireplace. Sive, Mike and Mena are in the kitchen.

Mike is seated by the fire. In his lap is a pony's collar much worn and patched. With a heavy bent shoemaker's needle he stitches a piece of sacking on it.

Sive is seated at the table at end furthest from Mike. Her satchel of books stands open on the table. Her head is bent over a book from which she is memorising sotto voce.

Mena stands over the working-table, her sleeves rolled up, her back turned to the other two. She is washing a shirt in a tin basin. She takes shirt from basin, squeezes it dry and places it on the table. She takes basin in her hand, goes to door, opens it and throws the dirty water out; closing the door she turns to Mike).

Mena:	The dogs are barking at the end of the bohareen. Someone is coming the road.
	(Mike does not look up from his work. Sive looks abstractedly towards Mena and then to her book again. Mena places the basin on the working table and pours some water into it from the drinking pail. She takes the shirt and begins to rinse it again in the basin. She turns as though to say something but changes her mind and continues with her washing. Sive closes the book, puts it in bag, takes another. She opens it and continues to memorise part of it).
	(There is a knock at the door. Mena goes to the door and asks).
Mena:	Who is out?
Voice:	(Off, sonorous, high-pitched). Thomasheen Sean Rua and Sean Dota from the butt of the hill. Doing a bit of rambling we are.
Mena:	Come in, let you!
	(The door opens and Thomasheen looks around the kitchen shiftily. He exchanges the barest of glances with Sive who looks at him curiously. He looks cautiously at Mike who ignores him, then at Mena who nods to him. Thomasheen turns and with a motion of his head calls Sean Dota. He enters the kitchen followed by Sean. Thomasheen makes straight for the fire and turns his back to it, lifting his coat-tails to warm himself).
Thomasheen:	(Shudders). God save all here. Brr! There is a cold there tonight that would peel the skin from your back. (To Sean Dota, in a mild pleasing tone). Come away in from the cold, Sean achree. there is a black wind coming around the shoulder of the mountain with fangs in it like the tooth of a boar.

(Sean Dota advances, shyly, a little ways. He looks for a moment gloatingly at Sive, and smiling shyly looks to Thomasheen. Sean is a small man, a little wizened. His age might be anything from 55 to 70. He takes off a bright-coloured cap and holds it supplicatingly in front of him. His hair is whitish-grey worn in a fringe at his fore head. His eyes are birdlike, shrewd. He wears a respectable frieze overcoat which seems too large for him).

Mena: You're welcome here, Sean Dota. Will you sit up to the fire and let the heat draw the cold out of your bones?

Sean Dota: No, thanks, Mrs. Glavin. I will sit here by the dresser. I'd not like to come in the way of anyone. *(His voice is apologetic. Whenever he speaks he also smiles with a half laugh as if to excuse himself. He sits on a chair by the dresser. He leans forward expectantly with his palms on his knees).*

Thomasheen: The heat don't agree with him. He would sooner a cold corner out of the way. *(Sean Dota nods with a half laugh in agreement with Thomasheen).* He have a very aisy-going manner with him. He have the health of a spring salmon, that man have. You wouldn't like to meet him, he's so nice. *(Sean Dota nods modestly).*

(Mike holds the collar out at arm's length to examine it. Thomasheen watches interestedly).

Thomasheen: You're a great hand for mendin'! There's a drop of the cobbler's blood in your veins, Mike, boy! 'Tis a joy to watch you with the needle. *(Mike gives him a withering look).*

Mike: *(To Mena).* Maybe they might have mind for a mouthful of tay?

Mena: The kettle is very near the boil.

(Sive begins to gather her books. Both of the new arrivals protest vigorously at the idea of tea).

Sean: We're only just after rising from the table. 'Twould be a waste. We're thankful, all the same.

Mena: 'Tis there in plenty if ye have a mind for it.

Thomasheen: Too good you are, woman, to put yourself out for us. *(He goes to the table and stands over Sive. He looks at the book in front of her. Then to the house at large he says).* Ah, the book-learning is a wonderful thing. Many is the time I have regrets for the idleness of my youth. What a nate Curate I would make, or a Canon, maybe, in time with the shoes shining by me night and morning. 'Tis a wise man that puts himself out for the learning. *(To Sive, cajolingly).* And what is it you have in the book there before you?

Sive: Poetry and verses.

Thomasheen: Ah! *(exhilaratingly).* Poetry ... God help us, 'tis far from the poetry book I was reared. There is a verse out of the end of a poem now, I heard a tinker woman reciting back the years. The way it goes ...

(He cocks his head and purses his lips, then in a stentorian voice almost bawdy in tone, he begins).

"The ripest apple is the soonest rotten;
The hottest love is the soonest cold ..."

(Out of the corner of his eye he surveys Sive).

"... and a young man's vows, they are soon forgotten;
Go away, young man, do not make so bold!"
Ah, poetry is a gift from the angels of Heaven!

(Mena squeezes the shirt, puts it aside, opens the door, and empties the basin).

Mike: *(Politely).* Have you a liking for the versifying, Sean?

14

	(Mena replaces the basin and folds her hands. She stands approvingly at the end of the kitchen behind Sive).
Sean Dota:	Divil the bit, Mike. I have nothing against the poets, mind you, but they are filled with roguery and they have the bad tongue on top of it, the thieves. Oh, the scoundrels!
Mena:	Have you e'er a poem, Sean? You must have great verses by you, a man with your gentlemanly nature.
Sean Dota:	Oho! *(Deprecatingly, laughs and shakes his head).*
Thomasheen:	Ah, he's as deep as a well, woman! As wise as a book! As sharp as a scythe! There's no telling the verses he have.
Mena:	Give us a rann out of one of them. I'll bet anything 'tis the best that was ever heard.
	(Sive is amazed at Sean's voice and manner. Sean looks at her keenly).
Sean Dota:	Begor, then, I will say a verse for the girl. It was from my grandfather I brought it.
	(Shifts on his seat). A very tasty handful of poetry too, it is.
	(He coughs, bringing his hand to his mouth delicately. In a sing-song voice, very high in tone, he starts).

'Seaneen Easter, di-do-dom,
Stole a pratey from his mom.
He was caught and he was hung.
He was buried in the dung.
When the dung was piking out
He was hopping like a trout.
When the dung was piking in
He was hopping like a hen."

	(Mena acclaims him loudly, as do Thomasheen and Mike. Sean shakes his head bashfully, giving the half-laugh again).
Mena:	*(Feigning delight).* Well, isn't he the devil's own!
Thomasheen:	Ah! he have the humour all over him.
Mike:	'Twas lively, faix!
	(Mike rises, having completed his work on the collar. He places it against the dresser and goes to his seat again).
Mena:	Sive, child *(gently)* there's a small journey for you. *(Full of supplication, she comes to where Sive is sitting. Her manner is pleading, yet considerate).* There's a favour. *(Pause).* Didn't the laths of the rail burst with the weight of turf. Would you by any chance go the road down to the butt of the bohareen to Seamus Donal's cottage. Tell him we want the loan of a rail for the morning. He is working in the quarry and sure he'll have no need of it himself. You can tell him it will be called for with the dawn.
Sive:	*(Resignedly).* I'll go!
Mena:	*(To the house in general).* She's a gift for obliging. *(Her voice is all praise).* She would turn on her heel from whatever she is at, to be of help. *(She helps Sive on with her coat).*
Sive:	*(Reflectively - looking up at Mena childishly).* To be called for at the dawn. I am to tell him the rail was burst with the weight of turf.
Mena:	And thank him for the use of it.
	(Sive goes to the dresser for her scarf).

Thomasheen: Well, it's a strange thing that I will be going home by the short cut across the mountain. It was only to keep me company on the road that Sean came as far as this with me. It would be nice for the girl to have his company as far as the foot of the bohareen.

(looking around with wide innocent eyes), and sure 'twould be company for him too. A young heart is a great companion on the road.

Sive: There is no need for Mr. Dota to come with me. I know the road well enough from walking it every day.

Thomasheen: Of course you do, who would know it better? *(Questions the company as if defying contradiction).* But think of the dark, girl, and the phuca *(Pauses)* the mad, red eyes of him like coals of fire lighting in his head. There is no telling what you would meet on a black road. There's a mad moon in the sky tonight with the stars out of their mind screeching and roaring at one another.

Sean Dota: *(Rises from the chair).* I'll be as far as Seamus Donal's with her. There will no one cross her path with Sean Dota walking by her side. *(Apologetic laugh).*

Sive: *(Indignantly).* I am not afraid of the dark, or the puca!

Thomasheen: Ah, sure, you would be like a hare on the road with the tidy little white feet of you.

Sean: It's as well to be going ... I have the notion of buying a motoring car *(to impress Sive).* It is all the fashion these days ... very saving on the feet. *(Again, the apologetic half-laugh).* By all accounts the women do be driving them, too.

(Sean leads the way out, followed by Sive who looks irritated at the thought of Sean's company).

Sean: Good night all, and God bless!

Thomasheen: Good night. God bless.

(Thomasheen runs silently to the door, opens it noiselessly and peeps out after them. Mena advances to the fire and stands at one side of it watching Thomasheen. Mike and Mena exchange glances. Thomasheen closes door and turns, rubbing hands gleefully).

Thomasheen: The seed is sown; the flower will blossom.

Mena: *(Sits opposite Mike and faces Thomasheen).* The old woman mustn't know ... the girl will know in good time ... No need to tell her. It will come over her like a summer tide.

(Thomasheen sits facing the fire and runs his fingers through his wild hair, head bent).

Mike: I can't folly with ye! If there was less between them in the years it would be a great day's work. She'll never take with him. It's too much to ask of her.

Mena: Are you forgetting the money? There is a soft bone somewhere in your head, man. And are you forgetting this evening and Liam Scuab.

Mike: I know! I know! The money is a great temptation but there is wrong in it from head to heel. Sive is young, with a brain by her. She will be dreaming about love with a young man. 'Tis the way the young girls do be!

Thomasheen: *(Comes nearer Mike and extends his hands).* Will you listen to him! Love! In the name of God, what do the likes of us know about love? *(Turns to Mena and points a finger at Mike).* Did you ever hear the word of love on his lips? Ah, you did not, girl! *(Thomasheen rises to the occasion).* Did he ever give you a little rub behind the ear or run his fingers through your hair and tell you that he would swim the Shannon for you. Did he ever sing the love-songs for you in the far-out part of the night when ye do be alone? *(Thomasheen scoffs).* he would sooner to stick his snout in a plate of mate and cabbage, or to rub the back of a fattening pig than whisper a bit of his fondness for you.

16

Do he run to you when he come in from the bog and put his arms around you and give you a big smohawnach of a kiss and tell you that the length of the day was like the length of a million years while he was separated from you? *(In triumph)*. Could you say that he ever brought you the token of a brooch or a bit of finery? ... Naa! More likely a few pence worth o' musty sweets if the drink made him foolish of a fair day. *(Scornfully)*. And to hear you bladderin' about love! The woman would think you were out of your mind if you put a hand around her on the public road. *(Mike looks hang-dog)*.

Mena: You are no one to talk!

Thomasheen: I make no boast either. What I say is what business have the likes of us with love? It is enough to have to find the bite to eat. When I was a young man, 20 years ago, my father, God rest him, put a finish to my bit of love.

Mena: *(In unbelief)*. You had love?

Thomasheen: I had a wish for a girl from the other side of the mountain. But what was the good when I had no place to take her. There was a frightful curam of us in my father's house with nothing but a sciath of spuds on the floor to fill us. I had two pigs fattening. *(Lonesome)*. My father was an amadawn, a stump of a fool who took his life by his own hand. He hung himself from a tree near the house. I swear to you he would never have hanged himself but he knew my two pigs would pay for his wake and funeral. 'Twas the meanness in his heart, for he knew well I had my heart set on marriage.

Mena: What a lonesome story you have for us?

Thomasheen: Not so lonesome now! There's a widow-woman having a small place beyond the village. 100 pounds would see me settled in with her.

Mike: She will be blessed by you! Will you give her the rub behind the ear? Will you give her brooches and clothes? Ha-ha! I would like to see it!

Thomasheen: Give over! ... *(To Mena)*. There is this young Scuab who have a heart for the girl. He will have fine words for her, looking like a gentleman, with his collar and tie and his poll plastered with hair-oil. *(Accent on "oil")*. I have seen him, after his day's work, looking like a play-actor.

Mena: No fear of him!

Thomasheen: He was in this house this evening!

Mena: You miss nothing!

Thomasheen: You'll have him coming into the house proposin' next! And it might interest you to know that she has been seen on at least one occasion, ducking out of here to meet Scuab after ye were gone to bed.

Mike: This is more serious than I thought and 'twill have to stop! I don't want her going the same road as her mother.

Mena: Then the old woman must know about it and never told us which means she is on their side and is probably even encouraging Sive in this. But there's one easy way to stop that sort of thing and that is to move Sive into the west room where I can keep my eye on her and her only means of coming and going will be through our bedroom.

Thomasheen: But that alone won't be enough! We must cut out every chance of their meeting. Scuab can still meet her and she comin' and goin' to school, so she must finish with her scoolin'. You can say you're no longer able to manage all the work by yourself, that you need her help, else ...

Mena: There is no fear of him, I tell you!

Mike: You're right, there is no fear of him. He will keep far away from here. But you will have a hard job with Sive.

17

Thomasheen: Will you listen to him cnabshealing again? He's never happy unless 'tis grumbling he is. Wouldn't you have the good word, anyway? You'd swear, to hear you talk, that we were all rogues and thieves. What are we trying to do only make an honest shilling. 'Tisn't going around stealing the dead out of their graves we are. 'Twould be a black day for us if we robbed a widow or stole a poor-box from the chapel. Isn't it only bringing two people together in wedlock we are?

Mena: When will he give the money?

Thomasheen: Sean Dota is only the half of a fool, not a full one! When the knot is tied, and not before. I have the night wasted in talking with ye. The cocks will be crowing by the time I'm home. *(He goes towards door and turns with his hand on latch).* A warning! *(He cocks his thumb towards the old woman's room).* Watch the oul' one up there! She have the makin's of trouble.·

(Exit Thomasheen Sean Rua. Mike rises, takes a cup from the dresser and goes to tankard. He takes off cover and dips cup, withdrawing it, he drinks with relish).

Mena: I would have made tea for you!

Mike: Tea is scarce enough without wasting it this hour of the night. *(He replaces cup, stretches his hands and yawns. He scratches his head roughly).* I have an early start in the morning and a hard day before me tomorrow. I think I'll go to the bed.

Mena: Will you not wait for Sive?

Mike: She will be all right. What can harm her? I have no heart somehow for looking her in the face.

Mena: I think I could sleep myself. *(She arranges fire with tongs while Mike unlaces and removes his boots).*

Mike: Would my mother have mind, do you think, for tea?

Mena: There is no fear of her! Hasn't she her pipe?

(Mena unlooses her hair, goes to lamp, and lowers wick. She turns and exits by door at side of hearth. Mike places his boots under the working table and in his socks crosses the kitchen and exits by the same door).

The kitchen is empty, eerie-looking in the bad light.

The door of the old woman's room opens and she enters the kitchen. She tiptoes to the door of her son's room and listens for a moment. Satisfied, she turns away and raises the wick of the lamp. She then sits at her place by the fire. She takes the tongs and re-makes the fire. With a look around her she unearths her pipe and thrusts it into her mouth. She finds matches and lights up. She sits thus for a moment or two. Suddenly the door opens and Sive enters. She leans against closed door and holds her hands to her breast, breathing heavily).

Nanna: Where were you until this hour of the night.

Sive: *(Unties her head scarf).* Down the bohareen at Seamus Donal's for the loan of a rail for Uncle Mike ... That old man, Sean Dota! Oh! *(She shakes her head and covers her face with her hands).*

Nanna: *(Querulously)* Sean Dota?

Sive: *(In disgust and fright).* He was on the road down with me. When we passed by the cumar near Donal's he made a drive at me! He nearly tore the coat off me. I ran into Donal's kitchen but he made no attempt to follow. Oh, the way he laughs *(in disgust)* like an ould sick thing. What is the meaning of it all, Gran?

Nanna: *(Draws upon her pipe, Sive sits near her).* 'Tis the nature of the man, child, no more! You will find that men are that way. Being old doesn't change them. It's nothing!

Sive:	He frightened the life out of me. I never expected it! *(Pause)*. You know, I think, Gran, it was a plan by them ... but it's so hard to believe.
Nanna:	It have the appearance of a plan ... Do you know what I think ... there are queer doin's goin' on between Mena and Thomasheen Rua ...

(Mena emerges from her room wearing a long nightdress reaching to her toes almost. The two start when they see her).

Mena:	*(Crossly; loudly)*. Are ye going to be there for the night gossiping! A nice thing for the nuns to learn about! Get away to bed out of that! Wasting oil, ye are. Go on! Clear away!

(Sive and Nanna rise. Sive hurries to her room. Nanna concealing the pipe in her palm, follows, slowly, and casts a defiant look at Mena. Exit Nanna and Sive. Mena rakes the fire again and quenches lamp altogether).

CURTAIN.

SCENE 3

A week later; late afternoon.

Nanna is at her usual place, Mena is kneading dough to make bread on the large table. A large jug of sour milk and a saucer of flour stand there. Mena lifts the dough and sprinkles flour on the board. She goes to flour bag, refills saucer with flour and returns to the table. She continues with the kneading, dusting the sodden bulk of it at times with flour. She turns her head towards the old woman.

Mena:	Is the pot ready?

(Nanna looks at a circular flat-bottomed pot near the fire).

Mena:	Is the hearing going by you, on top of everything else? Or is it how you're trying to rise the temper in me?
Nanna:	'Tis aisy enough to do that! The pot is as hot as ever 'twill be.
Mena:	And why wouldn't you say so? Sitting there, in the way of everyone!
Nanna:	Make your bread, woman! 'Tis hard enough to eat it without having to watch you
	baking it as well. 'Tis hard enough for a lonely old woman without a child to rock in the cradle.
Mena:	Ah, the back o' my hand to you for an oul' hag! There is no good in you - alluding and criticising always. Children bring nothing but misfortune. Didn't you see your own - the good end they came to. The gall of you, condemning me for my lack of child.

(Mena kneads the dough vigorously, smooths it in a circle, takes a knife from the cup boards and makes a cross on the top of the loaf. Taking a fist of flour she goes to the hearth and sprinkles the bottom of the pot. She returns to the table, takes the dough in her hands and places it in the pot. She takes the tongs and pushing the pot nearer the fire, arranges coals around it. She takes a cloth from the cupboard and cleans the table).

Mena:	Keep an eye to the bread. I'm going out to give hay to the cows.

Nanna:	*(Pointedly)*. Are you sure it is the cows you are going to see? Are you sure it isn't making mischief you're going?
Mena:	*(Crossly)*. What is behind that?
Nanna:	Well enough you know what is behind it.
Mena:	Come out with what you have to say. Don't be going around in circles like a salmon in a pool.
Nanna:	Fine words!
Mena:	Is it how you're so twisted inside of you that you must have the double meaning the whole time?
Nanna:	I will have what meaning I like! God gave me my tongue, not you!
Mena:	Now when you are meaning me, will you have strange meanings. What is behind your words?
Nanna:	That the heart might wither up in your breast - you know what is behind my words. What is the secrecy between yourself and Thomasheen Sean Rua? What is bringing the old man, Sean Dota, here, day in day out? Will you have the gall to answer?
Mena:	*(Indignant)*. What has it to do with you?
Nanna:	It is my grand-daughter that is concerned.
Mana:	*(Throws back her head and scoffs)*. Your grand-daughter ... and do you know, old woman, who her father is? Maybe you will tell? Thanking me from her heart, she should be, the fine match I am making for her. Putting myself out to place her in a gentleman's house.
Nanna:	Suiting yourself you are, like you always did.
Mena:	*(Viciously)*. Go to hell!
	(There is a knock on the door).
Mena:	Come in, let you!
	(Enter Thomasheen Sean Rua. He gives the customary furtive glance around the kitchen, his eyes coming to rest on the old woman. Mena nods encouragingly to him and he advances, leaving door open behind him).
Nanna:	Was there no door in the last house you were in?
Thomasheen:	*(Carrying an ashplant, hoists it dexterously in his hand)*. The deaf ear is the only cure for your equals ... *(then, to Mena)*. You will have company shortly, I am thinking. *(Goes to door, looks out to his right and turns again)*.
Mena:	Who is on the road?
Thomasheen:	Father and son, but brothers likewise, since the pair of them are sons of the devil.
Mena:	Who is that?
Thomasheen:	Two tinker-men ... Pats Bocock and his son, Cathalawn. Two robbers who have no liking for me or any of mine.
Nanna:	Dacent poor people with no home of their own. Good friends when they are needed.
Thomasheen:	You know your own! But I know them as rogues! They would cut my gad because I have great call at the matchmaking.
Nanna:	I would be proud to own them. *(Eyes Mena coldly)*. They are visiting here with many a year.

20

Mena: With the hands out and the mouths open, by them. Nothing more and nothing less than beggars.

Nanna: They are the people of the road - travelling people. They are above the class beggar.

(In the distance is the sound of a bodhran and a voice singing. The sound increases while the occupants of the kitchen await Pats Bocock and Carthalawn.

The air of the song is that of "Neath The Bright Silvery Light of the Moon" - the Irish ballad not to be confused with "By the Light of the Silvery Moon", the American bal lad. The words of the song are impromptu and created by Carthalawn.

(N.B. - the same air will persist in all his songs throughout the remainder of the play).

Enter Carthalawn and Pats Bocock. They keep step with each other. Pats is dressed in an ancient swallowtail coat and ancient trousers with strong boots. His hat is normal but the hollow in the crown is pushed upwards to give it the gaudy appearance of a top hat. He carries a stout blackthorn stick which he taps on the floor with each step. His left leg is shorter than his right and he walks with a lop-sided motion. He is of stern appearance but looks poverty-stricken nevertheless.

His son, Carthalawn, wears a short coat and is otherwise dressed as his father. In short, his dress is typical of the southern tinker who never wears a collar and tie, who has a jaunty air of good health about him but is above all hard to face. He carries a small bodhran.

What is important about the pair is that both of them keep the same step like soldiers on the march, and have an understanding between each other.

Entering the kitchen both men come to a halt before the large table. Pats strikes the floor with his stick and taking up the rhythm Carthalawn taps the bodhran with his knuckles.

He strikes loudly at first, then gently with a very low rubbing of knuckles, preparatory to singing.

Nanna rises to her feet, as is the custom when travelling minstrels enter a house, because the first song must be in praise of the man of the house, who is generally absent at work in the fields.

As the sound of the bodhran decreases, the tapping of Pat's stick becomes stronger. Then suddenly the tapping of stick and sound of bodhran become extremely faint and Carthalawn begins his song. His voice is bell-like in tone. The accent is slightly nasal.

Carthalawn: *(Singing):* Oh! Mike Glavin, you're the man;
You was always in the van;
With a dacent house to old man and gorsoon;
May white snuff be at your wake,
Bakers bread and curan - y cake
And plinty on your table, late and soon.

(Nanna applauds the song, while Mena and Thomasheen are indifferent. Pats advances and shakes hands with Nanna).

Pats: *(Deep voiced and solemn with unsmiling face).* 'Tis not aisy, a-girl, to kill you! You have the appearance of a small one, a young one. We do be praying for you in our prayers, whenever we get the notion to kneel. (*He turns to Mena).* God bless you, bean a'-tighe, with your fine appearance and your name for generosity. (*Pats shakes hands with Mena. Her reaction is dismal and suspicious. Pats ignores her indifference and extends his hand to Thomasheen who turns his back to Pats).*

Nanna: *(In a loud voice, full of warning).* You are as well off, Pats, without the paw of the devil burning your palm.

21

(Pats returns to his son's side; both stand rigid).

Mena: What is it ye want?

Pats: No more than a dorn of sugar and a dusteen of tea. We have the caravan beyant in the steamrolled road. Liam Scuab *(he bends his head in thanks while Carthalawn stands rigid),* a dacent man, gave us the side of a loaf. We have our own accoutrements. If there is the giving of tea and sugar we will thank the hand that gives it. If there is not, maybe there is the giving of a silver piece. Is there anything from Thomasheen Sean Rua of the mountain - making it in plenty he is.

(Pat extends his palm to Thomasheen who has turned again to face him).

Thomasheen: *(Slightly panicky).* Where would the likes of me come by silver money? There is the half of the country looking for men to work in the bogs. Why should a man beg when there is work before and after him?

Nanna: There is no luck in refusing a man of the road!

(Pats looks with hard eyes at Thomasheen, who surveys him with superiority, both hands held behind back. Pats opens his mouth and throws back his head in a dangerous fashion. Tapping his stick on the floor, he makes a circuit of the table to where Carthalawn stands. He stands by his son's side still tapping).

Pats: Your best! Your mighty best!

(Violently Pats begins to tap his stick upon the floor. Carthalawn looks upward at the ceiling and begins to tap the bodhran with clenched knuckles. For a moment there is loud timing of stickbeat and bodhran. Then the sound dwindles and Carthalawn takes up the beat to his usual air, while the stick is pointed at Thomasheen).

Carthalawn: *(Still at "attention", addresses himself to Thomasheen while his father stands at "attention").*

> May the snails devour his corpse,
> And the rain do harm worse;
> May the devil sweep the hairy creature soon;
> He's as greedy as a sow;
> And the crow behind the plough;
> That black man from the mountain, Seaneen Rua!

(Pats stamps both his legs and his stick with delight. Nanna crows with aged laughter. Thomasheen turns his back again, boiling with impotent rage. Carthalawn, having fulfilled his duty, stands unsmiling).

Nanna: I will give ye the grain o'tay and sugar out of respect to yeer singing.

(Mena immediately goes and takes her stand between Nanna and the dresser).

Mena: *(Like a guard at arms).* You will give nothing! Is it how you think that tea and sugar are made by wishing?

Thomasheen: *(Turning around viciously)* - Arrah, that's right! Give nothin'! *(Pronounced "Notten").* Give nothin!! *(He cranes his neck forward).* The smart men o' the roads. Goin' around criticizin' dacent men an' women. *(Thomasheen advances a step, assured of Mena's help).* Tea and sugar, how are you? The cheek of the two biggest robbers walking the roads of Ireland.

(Pats and Carthalawn back towards the door, fearful of their grounds. Thomasheen, thinking he has gained the ascendancy, follows up his victory. Pats and Carthalawn stand in line with the door).

Thomasheen: *(Confident).* Will ye look at the appearance of them! A short leg and a half-fool! Two with the one word, goin' around with their songs, frightenin' half the country. Go on away to yeer smelly caravan and not be disgustin' respectable people!

(Thomasheen draws back his right hand as if to strike them. As he does so, Pats taps again with his stick. Carthalawn knuckles the bodhran. Both assume ritual dignity to the rhythm of bodhran and blackthorn).

Pats: *(To Carthalawn).* Carthalawn, your best! Your Almighty best! *(With temper he keeps tapping. Imperiously he points stick at Thomasheen as in a ritual from time immemorial. Carthalawn sings slowly, his voice bell-like and piercing. The tapping and the bodhran grow quieter).*

Carthalawn: *(Sings):*   On the road from Abbeyfeale,
Sure I met a man with meal,
Come here, said he, and pass your idle time;
On me he made quite bold
Saying the young will wed the old
And the old man have the money for the child.

(Thomasheen turns to look to Mena who stands helpless. Pats taps his stick loudly on the floor with appreciation, full of smiles and headshaking. Nanna crows with delight simultaneously. Thomasheen returns to where Mena stands barring Nanna's way to the dresser. Mena folding her hands over her bosom in a fighting attitude, advances until she faces Carthalawn and his father).

Mena: You brought your story well! *(To Pats).* Come out with what you have to say. Don't be hiding behind the words of a half-fool, *(indicating Carthalawn).*

Pats: 'Tis the talk of the country that Sean Dota the farmer is marrying a young girl out of this house. If their tales are true her name is Sive. The people are saying that it is a strange match that a young girl who is at the start of her days should marry an old man who is at the end of his. They say he is struggling to keep the spark of life inside of him. They say she is the flower of the parish.

Mena: How dare you cast your aspersions under this roof?

Pats: *(Calmly).* 'Tis only what the people are saying! *(He points his stick at Thomasheen).* They say he is the man who brought it about; that he will score well out of it. 'Tis only what the people are saying; *(roguishly).* That is the common word everywhere our feet take us.

Mena: And what is it to them or to you either, the way we conduct ourselves? Is it the first time a young girl marries a man older than her? She is matching well for herself.

Pats: There is no one saying otherwise.

Nanna: The devil's work, that's what it is!

Pats: We will come calling the night of the wedding.

Thomasheen: There will be nothing here for ye.

Pats: We will come all the same, welcome or not!

Nanna: There was always welcome here for Pats Bocock.

Pats: 'Tis the changing of the times.

Thomasheen: *(To Pats).* 'Twill be a good change when the likes of ye do a day's work. Into jail ye should be put, a brace of dirty beggars.

Pats: *(Full of venom).* I'm listening to you, Thomasheen Sean Rua and I'm watching you and I'm telling you what you are. You are the bladder of a pig, the snout of a sow; you are the leavings of a hound, the sting of a wasp. You will die roaring. Carthalawn! Your best! Your almighty best!

(Pats stands rigid and taps the stick. Carthalawn knuckles bodhran, volume is reduced and Carthalawn sings as both men turn for the door in step).

23

Carthalawn: *(Singing):* May the snails devour his corpse
And the rain do harm worse;
May the devil sweep the hairy creature soon;

(They go out, but the singing is heard, growing fainter).

He's as greedy as a sow;
And the crow behind the plough;
That black man from the mountain, Seaneen Rua!

(Thomasheen goes to the door and closes it after Pats and Carthalawn. Flexing the stick with his hands behind his back, he glares at Nanna).

Thomasheen: Who has been broadcasting my private affairs around the countryside. *(With Nanna alone he is confident again and bent upon cowarding her).* You are a lone woman with your husband feeding worms in his trench. You have terrible gumption with no one left to back you.

Mena: Go on, you oul' wretch ... Answer the man ... Where is your stiffness gone to?

Thomasheen: Go on! Say it, you oul' hag! Aaaah! You'll say nothin' now. Face the end of your days, oul' woman!

Nanna: Ye had little to say a while back, either of ye, when the composing was going on. I will tell my son when he comes home the way ye are at me.

Mena: Little your son cares about you. Long ago you should have been put in your place. Small thanks you show for the freedom you have here. Would it not enter your head that there is many an oul' woman of your age walking the road without a roof above or a bed beneath them.

Thomasheen: Sure the County Home is filled to the jaws with the likes of her. You will see the crowds of them sticking their heads out of the windows watching the visitors coming and going and they hoping that someone will come to take them away out of it. 'Tis the sport of Cork to see the way they do be haggling and scraping over the few potatoes and the forkful of meat. (Solemnly). Ah, but sure the hardest of all, God pity us, is that they will stop the oul' women of smoking. An oul' lady from the other side of the mountain that used to have a liking for her pipe of tobaccy went out of her mind after three days. She would be heard screeching in the other world. They had a piece of sacking over her mouth to keep her quiet but sure that was no good but as little. She started scraping her self till the flesh hung from her in gibbles and the blood used to be coursin' down out of her in streams. 'Twas a madness for the pipe, you see! *(Sanctimoniously).* She was a terrible sight when she died. They buried her in the middle of the night with not a living Christian in the world of her own people to say a prayer for her ... Aah! Some people do not know when they are well off!

Mena: She will change!

Thomasheen: She have the appearance of one that won't!

Mane: She'll change! She's enough of a burden without becoming a curse altogether.

Thomasheen: Walking the road she should be like the rest of her equals.

Mena: Will she walk the road? ... Far from it ... Where is the independent woman we had in her? *(Mena lifts latch and opens doors. She indicates the world beyond with a flourish).* Go on, if you have the mind for it! *(Shouts).* Go on and put your bag on your back and go begging from door to door. Will she go, do you think? ... will she? ... No! nor go! What a fool she would be to leave her warm fire with the pipe handy by her and the good table with her three rounds of diet every day.

Nanna: *(To the fire).* There is a hatchery of sin in this house. *(Her voice is full of defeat).*

(Mena bounces forward till she is close to Nanna. Thomasheen advances likewise).

24

Mena:	(Violently). No more of your sharp answers, you oul' wretch. You sit there, day in, day out, taking all you can get without a word of thanks. You will have a puss by you like the child in the cot feeding yourself up with the fruits of our labours, taking all as if you were born for it, like the queen of the land.
Nanna:	(Repeats). "Like a child in the cradle". (Shakes her head pitifully).
Mena:	(Stiffens with rage). Is it my fault that your son is a tired gomeril of a man?
Nanna:	A cluckin' hen won't hatch!
Mena:	(Advances and draws back her hand). I will strike you. (Full of venom). I will take the head from your shoulders.

(Mena draws back her hand again to strike a blow. Thomasheen drops his stick, inter venes promptly, and drags Mena back towards the door, she struggles in his grasp, to have at Nanna, but he holds her firmly).

Thomasheen:	(From behind Mena, still holding her, to Nanna). See what you're after doing? (Guilefully). You have her upset. (To Nanna). You will answer for your evil soul...
Mena:	She'll burn! she'll burn the day she gives over life!
Thomasheen:	(To Nanna). Don't be goadin' her! Don't be goadin' her.
Nanna:	(Having crossed to her bedroom door, Nanna turns). I'll say it again. There's a hatchery of sin in this house.

(When she has gone, Thomasheen releases his hold on Mena who looks with murderous intent towards the room into which Nanna has entered).

Thomasheen:	Leave her be for the now. The mind for fight is gone from her. (He stoops, and retrieves his stick, and makes small circles on the floor with its point). There is a play to all things. D'you see th' oul' cock salmon that do be hidin' in the deep hole of the river They will be firing stones at him and making plans for his capture. They will be poisoning and making the use of nets but they might as well be idle. (Is very positive) 'Tis the age that will do the work. 'Tis the mounting up of the years. Aaah! age is a killin's thief! Age is the boy that will stand no nonsense. He have a grip like a double-knot ... The old woman is tiring.

(Pause).

Mena:	When will he give the money?
Thomasheen:	If there is a wedding, 'twill be on the morning of the wedding, on the word of a man. Is there any word out of the girl.
Mena:	She will do what is to be done. Am I to be telling you forever?
Thomasheen:	But have she said the word out of her mouth?
Mena:	What is the need for that?
Thomasheen:	It would put my mind more at ease.
Mena:	Well, you can rest your mind, She will marry Sean Dota and that will be the end of it.
Thomasheen:	'Tis a fine thing to hear the good word anyway. Still I may tell you I will not rest happy till he has the halter on her.
Mena:	(Raises a hand to Thomasheen to ensure silence - she listens a moment). That will be Sive now. When she comes in, pass her the time of day - no more; then go away about your business and leave the rest in my hands. 'Tis work for a woman now.
Thomasheen:	(Hurries to window and looks out). You will put the best things before her.
Mena:	Gather yourself and be ready to go.
Thomasheen:	What about? ... (He points to Nanna's room).

Mena: She'll dance to my tune ... Aisy!

(The latch lifts and Sive enters. She is dressed as before and carries the satchel of books in her hand. She looks from Mena To Thomasheen, frowns for the barest fraction of a second, and lays her satchel on the table. She undoes her headscarf and lays it across the satchel).

Thomasheen: *(Sweetly).* Is the schoolin' over for today with ye?

Sive: *(To Mena).* The bicycle got punctured again. I had to walk from beyond the cross.

Thomasheen: I will have to be going. There is a great length coming to the days, thanks be to God. We will have the summer now down on the door before we know.

Mena: Good-bye to you, Thomasheen.

Thomasheen: *(Nods politely to Sive, who edges away to let him pass).* I will be seeing ye again, please God, before we're older.

Mena: *(Impatiently).* We will be here! *(Inclination of head).*

(Thomasheen twirls his stick and opens the door).

Thomasheen: *(Airily).* Good luck, all.

(When he has gone, Mena takes one of the buckets from under working-table and pours water from the drinking pail into it. She replaces the drinking pail. Mena then scoops several fistfuls of meal from the bag into the bucket).

Sive: *(Hesitant).* The tubes of the bicycle are full of holes.

(Mena dries her hands on her apron and turns to Sive).

Mena: *(Sympathetically).* We will have to do something about it, for sure. I will tell himself to be on the look for a pair of new tubes in the village. Will I wet a mouthful o' tea for you while you're waiting for the dinner. *(Sive is too surprised to reply).* There is a piece of sweet cake I have put away. You must be tired after your day.

Sive: *(Befuddled).* No ... no ... don't bother with the tea! I'll wait until the dinner.

Mena: A cup of milk, so! *(without waiting for reply, she hurries to dresser, takes a cup, fills it and forces it on Sive).* It must be an ease for you to get away from the nuns and the books, but sure we won't have much more of the schooling now.

(Gently Mena forces Sive to a chair near the table. Sive places the cup before her and looks bewilderedly at Mena at the word "school");

Mena: Any of the girls in the parish would give their right hand to have the chance that's before you.

Sive: But ...

Mena: *(Quickly before Sive can reply).* Don't think about it now. think of the handling of thousands and the fine clothes and perfumery. Think of the hundreds of pounds in Creamery cheques that will come in the door to you and the servant boy and the servant girl falling all over you for fear you might dirty your hands with work.

Sive: *(Shakes her head several times as though to ward off Mena's words).* You don't know ... you ... you ...

Mena: Sit down now and rest yourself. You could have your grandmother with you. Think of the joy it would give the poor woman to have the run of such a fine house ... and to see you settled there. 'Tis a fine thing for you, my girl and sure, what matter if he's a few years older than you. Won't we be all old in a handful of short years? Ah! I would give my right hand to be in your shoes.

Sive: *(Shakes her head continually).* Please, please ... you don't know what you are saying. How can you ask me such a thing?

26

Mena:	Now, tomorrow himself will call to the convent and tell the Reverend Mother that you will not be going in any more. What would a grown-up woman like you want with spending your days in the middle of children.
Sive:	I could never live with that old man. *(Entreats Mena)*. Fancy the thought of waking in the light of day and looking at him with the small head of him. Oh, my God! No! I could never! ... I could not even think of it!
Mena:	*(Still motherly)*. Nonsense, child! That is nothing. Have sense for yourself. I know what you are going into. Do you think I would not gainsay him if it wasn't the best thing for you. *(Places a hand around Sive's shoulder)*. Sit here, child, and drink your milk.
	(Mena gently brings Sive to the chair, seats her and stands behind her with both hands resting lightly on Sive's shoulders. Mena's face becomes shrewd. Sive looks vacantly before her - towards the audience).
Mena:	Will you picture yourself off to the chapel every Sunday in your motor-car with your head in the air and you giving an odd look out of the window at the poor oinsheacs in their donkey-and-cars and their dirty oul' shawls and their faces yellow with the dirt by them. Will you thank God that you won't be for the rest of your days working for the bare bite and sup like the poor women of these parts.
Sive:	*(Raises her head and entwines her hands)*. Imagine what the girls at school would say! Imagine going to a dance with him, or going up the chapel with him!
Mena:	All I know is that you will be independent. You will have no enemy when you have the name of money.
Sive:	I don't know what to think or to say. I do not want to give offence, but I will never marry such a man. I will not marry at all!
Mena:	*(Motherly again)*. You will change! You will change when you think by yourself of the misery you are leaving; when you think of the way you were born.
	(Sive eagerly turns and looks innocently at Mena. She is changed suddenly to an eager girl awaiting the solution of a problem that has for a long time baffled her).
Sive:	Surely you don't remember when I was born. *(Her eyes widen as she looks at Mena. For the first time she takes an interest in Mena's soliloquy)*. Nobody ever told me about my father or mother or what sort of people they were.
	(Sive looks into Mena's face searching for the truth).
Mena:	I will tell the tale. Himself would never bring himself to say it. You would think it was some kind of a blemish that should be hidden and sure, what was it, only the work of nature. Your mother, God grant her a bed in heaven, was a nice lie of a girl. Your father took himself away quickly out of these parts and, if he is alive, never made himself known. There was no blame to your mother, God help her. Your grandmother, for all yeer talking and whispering behind my back, was never the one to come out with the truth.
Sive:	But my father ... wasn't he drowned in England?
Mena:	Your father was never a father, God forgive him. he straightened his sails and disappeared like the mist of a May morning. It was no wonder your mother died with the shame of it. No blame, achree! *(With feeling then)*. No blame to what is mortal. Do you think it is how two people will stay apart forever who have blood becoming a flood in their veins. It is the way things happen ... *(conviction)* ... the sound of fiddles playing airy hornpipes, the light of a moon on the pale face of a river, the whispered word ... the meeting of soft arms and strong arms ... *(pauses)* ...
Sive:	I thought you said you'd tell me about my father.
Mena:	*(Unaccountably vexed)*. I'm telling you your father was nothing. He was no father. He had no name. You have no name. You will have no name till you take a husband. Do

27

you see the hungry greyhound or the mongrel dog? It is the same way with a man. It is no more than the hunger. It is time you were told, my girl. You are a bye-child, a common bye-child - a bastard!

(Sive attempts to rise. Mena roughly pushes her back in the chair).

Mena: You will sleep with that old woman no longer. *(She flings the schoolbag across the room).* There will be no more school for you. School is a place for schoolmasters and children. Every woman will come to the age when she will have a mind for a room of her own. I mind when I was a child, when I was a woman, there were four sisters of us in the one room. There was no corner of a bed we could call our own. We used to sit into the night talking and thieving and wondering where the next ha'penny would come from or thinking would it ever come to our turn to meet a boy that we might go with, and be talking with and maybe make a husband out of. We would kill *(vexed)*. We would beg, borrow or steal. We would fire embers of fire at the devil to leave the misery of our own house behind us, to make a home with a man, any man that would show four walls to us for his time in the world. *(In a voice of warning).* Take no note of the man who has nothing to show for himself, who will be full of rameish and bladder, who would put wings on ould cows for you but has no place to make a marriage bed for you. Take heed of a man with a piece of property. He will stand over his promise. He will keep the good word for you because he has the keeping of words ... Now go to the room and be sure to think of what I said.

(Sive rises instinctively goes towards her own room but remembering, turns and exits by the far door to Mena's bedroom).

END OF ACT 1.

ACT TWO

SCENE ONE

(Mena sits at the table preparing the shopping list for the wedding. There is a knock on the door).

Mena:	*(Listens a moment).* Come in!
	(Enter Liam Scuab. He looks around the kitchen).
Mena:	You have the devil's own gall coming here. Lucky for you that Mike is away.
Liam:	I don't give a hatful of bornacks for Mike or for you either. I come here to see Sive.
Mena:	What do you want Sive for?
Liam:	I want to talk with her.
Mena:	You put a journey on yourself for nothing. Sive isn't here. *(Turning away to re-arrange fire).*
Liam:	How is it her bike is up against the wall of the house?
Mena:	*(Angry).* Are you telling me she's here? Are you making a liar out of me in my own house?
Liam:	I didn't call you a liar. I only thought you might be making a mistake.
Mena:	*(Loudly).* Same thing, isn't it? Didn't I say she wasn't here?
Liam:	There's no harm if I wait for her so. I won't be in your way.
Mena:	You have no business here. If Mike finds you there will be war. You're not wanted in this house. Clear off on your road and don't be vexing me.
Liam:	I have no wish to make an enemy out of you. I will wait till he comes.
Mena:	*(Violently).* Will you have your own way in all things, will you? Will you be coming into people's houses causing trouble. Get away out of here Or I'll get the tongs to you.
Liam:	I love her!
Mena:	*(Mimicking).* You love her! You do! You love her! You gomaill.
	(There is a sound without, and Mike enters).
Mena:	Look, what's before you! Look at him and don't blame me, because he wouldn't go for me.
Mike:	*(In overcoat with cap, places sack and whip aside and throws cap on table).* I see him! *(Mike sits on the sacks).*
Liam:	I mean no harm, Mike Glavin, to you or your wife.
Mike:	*(Taking off his boots).* What do you want, Scuab?
Liam:	I want to see Sive.
Mike:	*(Mutters thoughtfully).* You came to see Sive, did you? Sive, faith, of all ones! What do you want to see her for, Scuab?
Liam:	To have a talk with her.
Mike:	*(Calmly).* No, you'll have no talk with her.
Liam:	Only for a moment.

Mike:	She's in my care. You'll have to talk with me.
Liam:	I know you won't heed me but I was told that Sive was getting married.
Mike:	Who told you that?
Liam:	The two tinkers, Carthalawn and Pats Bocock. They were singing a song. It was easy to read the news.
Mena:	Now for sure you're a fool, when you pay attention to the grunting of pigs.
Liam:	They make sense in their own way.
Mike:	'Tis nonsense.
Liam:	If it is nonsense, so, tell me why is Thomasheen Sean Rua, the matchmaker, coming here every day and often twice in the day?
Mike:	He has how own business with me. You're like a magistrate with your foxy digs at us.
Liam:	Alright, so, but what is the reason for another thing?
Mike:	What other thing?
Liam:	The old man, Sean Dota, the farmer, he is coming here every day now too.
Mike:	Is he now, and what do you make out of it all?
Liam:	I have heard him talking to himself on the road.
Mena:	Talking to himself, will you tell us?
Liam:	I have heard him.
Mena:	And what does he be saying?
Liam:	Things about Sive, and how he will warm her before she is much older. A lot of other things, too, but most of it not fit to mention again.
Mike:	*(Crossly)*. So what if he does? What is it to you?
Liam:	I know he will marry Sive.
	(Mike and Mena exchange shrewd looks).
Mike:	Ah, yerra, you're going farther from sense with every word.
Mena:	Sure, isn't that what I told him.
Liam:	It's hard to believe it could be true.
Mike:	There is no truth at all to it, man.
Liam:	Oh, for God's sake, will the two of you stop treating me like a child. The whole parish knows what's going on. It is the talk at every crossroads that Sive is match-making with Sean Dota. In the village the public-houses are full with the mockery of it.
Mike:	*(Advancing a step)*. I've come to the last sod with you, Scuab. Get out of this house before I be tempted to take a weapon in my hands. *(Clenches fists)*. You'd better be going, Scuab, or I'll take the whip to you.
Mena:	And I the tongs. I'll put streaks on you worse than a raddle-stick.
Liam:	*(Pleads)*. In the honour of God, I beseech you to forget about violence. I tell you I want no trouble. If I have upset ye, I'm sorry, but surely if ye know God ye must think of this terrible auction. Ye must know that a day will dawn for all of us when an account must be given. Do not think of me. I promise I will leave these parts till Sive is a woman. I swear that on my dead mother. But do not give her to that rotting old man with his gloating eyes and trembling hands.
Mike:	*(Less angrily)*. Enough, Scuab! Go! *(Turns aside)*.

Mena:	Wasn't it one of your breed that blackened her mother's name, wasn't it? Oh, the cheek of you, you upstart out of the gutter.
Liam:	Think, woman, I beg of you! Think, Mike Glavin! Forget about yourselves and see it with good eyes instead of greedy ones. Have you knowledge of the Crucified Son of God? *(Shakes his head with emotion).* Are you forgetting Him who died on Calvary? Are you forgetting the sorrow and terrible sadness of His bloody Face as He looks at ye now? Will ye stand and watch each other draw the hard crooked thorns deep into His helpless body?
Mena:	*(Violent temper).* Gerraway our-a that! Get away!
Liam:	*(Backing towards door).* Nothing in Heaven or Hell could move ye to see wrong!
	(Mena whips the sharp knife off the dresser).
Mena:	I'll open you! I'll open you if you vex me more.
Liam:	I'm going. You'll live to remember this night.
	(Exit Liam. Mena scowlingly replaces knife and looks at Mike who stands sullen).
Mena:	What's wrong with you now?
Mike:	Nothing!
Mena:	Well, put a stir on yourself. You have a priest to see.
Mike:	*(Sighs).* Aye!
	(Enter Sive looking a little wan).
Sive:	I thought I heard the voice of Liam Scuab.
Mena:	You thought right! He was here.
Sive:	What was he looking for?
Mena:	He's a strange one! He came wishing you joy. You'd never think he would. He wished you joy and plenty on your wedding.
Sive:	*(In astonishment).* He wished me joy and plenty!
Mena:	*(Nods).* And he'll pray for your happiness and he's going away altogether to foreign places. That is the last we'll see of him, God help us. That the blessing of God go with him!
Sive:	*(In wonder).* Did he say any more?
Mena:	*(To Mike).* Did he say any more?
Mike:	Mmmmm!
Mena:	Divil the word more, only to turn on his heel as airy as you please and off with him.
Sive:	He's gone for good? *(turns towards room).* To think that he's gone for good.
Mena:	Gone, he is!
Sive:	*(Tearfully).* Oh! Liam could never do a thing like that.
	(She turns with her hands to her face and exits).
Mena:	There 'tis all now settled and no more to it.
Mike:	She has no heart for it.
Mena:	She'll have heart in time. 'Twill be nothing at all when she gets settled in for herself. What way was I when I came to this house? No one to say a good word for me and amn't I coming into my own now in spite of all?
Mike:	That was a different story? You were wanting to get married. Sive has no wish for it.

32

Mena:	*(Crossly)*. Are you at it again? Snamhshealin'? It was different in no way. How was it different? With an oul' devil in the corner screechin' at me the length of the day and a dirty brat of an orphan bawling in the corner.
Mike:	Sive is young!
Mena:	*(Indignantly)*. And wasn't I young?
Mike:	I know! I know! But ...
Mena:	But this, and but that! I'm going for a bucket of water to the well. You can eat, if you want it.
Mike:	I'll shave if I'm to see the priest.
Mena:	*(Taking bucket)*. there's water in the kettle for you.
	(Exit Mena).
Mike:	I can eat a bite when I'm done.
	(Mike takes brush, soap and an open razor and places them on working table. He fetches kettle and pours water into basin on table, finds towel in cupboard and sets about softening his bristle).
	(Enter Nanna silently. She is on her way to her chair by the fire when her movement is arrested by a sudden thought. She turns).
Nanna:	What are you shaving for at this hour of the day? Is it Sunday or Monday we have?
Mike:	*(Without turning)*. Is it a sin to shave? Must I answer for everything?
Nanna:	*(Tone of menace)*. You will answer for enough in your own time.
	(Mike spins around suddenly, holding soap and brush in hands).
Mike:	And what is this, all of a sudden?
Nanna:	There is a curse of evil on this house. Your dead sister and my dead daughter will curse it from her grave.
Mike:	*(Wearily, irritably)*. Will ye never stop pestering me.
Nanna:	There was never an ounce of luck in this house since that greasy bitch darkened the door of it.
Mike:	*(Dangerously)*. You mean, who?
Nanna:	I mean that hungry sow that sleeps with you. I mean that pauperized wretch you call a wife.
Mike:	You never had a good word for her. She's my wife and she'll always be that. A man's wife will always be his wife, let them both be what they will.
Nanna:	Far be it from me to spoil your home and put ye fighting. But surely you must give an ear to the word of your own mother that suckled you when you were a tiny boy, that watched over you like a hawk, that kept the wind and the rain away from you. *(Near to tears)*. Surely you will listen to your own mother that loved you as no one ever will.
Mike:	*(Weary, considerate)*. What ails you, mother ... what ails my mother?
Nanna:	Sive, Mike, Sive! Poor Sive! What are ye doing to her? Is there no heart in you at all?
Mike:	*(Head averted)*. 'Tis for the best, I tell you. 'Tis for the best.
Nanna:	'Tis for the best that she marry an ould fooleen of a man! Mike, you will not look at me in the face and say 'tis for the best! Will you look at me in the face, my son!
Mike:	Are you trying to drive nails into me? What am I to do? Do you want to have she be like her poor mother? Don't you know that Scuab has an eye for her?

33

Nanna:	Liam Scuab is a good boy. He would make a good husband. There is lies to you, Mike!
Mike:	Did his cousin make a good husband for Sive's mother? Will you have her conceiving again under sin? Will you have another Scuab do bad work?
Nanna:	That is a wrong thing to say, leanav! Oh! 'tis a wrong thing. Sive and Liam Scuab will not wear under temptation. There is a sweet thing in their love. Shame to you, Mike!
Mike:	Will you forget so quick? Quick was Liam Scuab's cousin when he reneged your daughter. Quick was he after his days and nights of pleasure. Quick was my sister's death. Quick is death, mother! *(Losing control).* Quick is marriage and quick is love and quick is youth. Quick is Sive's womanhood before we know it. We can't ask all things nice, mother. The nicest of things happen quick, likewise the worst things. Quick is the best thought and thing of a man and gone before he knows it. Sive is lucky. She marries young with nothing to bear. She is only a girl and lucky, not a woman who will have been thinking of men.
Nanna:	How is it all men will find words to save themselves? *(Sadly).* Women must pay for all happiness. That is their sorry shape, God help us.
Mike:	*(Embarrassed).* Go aisy, mother!
Nanna:	How can I go aisy when my own grandchild is for sale like an animal.
Mike:	*(Shouts).* Am I to have no rest from ye? Are ye to be pricking and prodding always?
	(Mike opens the towel and places the soap, razor and brush in it. He folds the towel about them. He opens the front door to the yard. He takes the basin in one hand and the towel in the other, all in a passionate temper).
Mike:	I will shave in the stable. There will be no nagging there!
	(Exit Mike. Slowly Nanna rises and closes the door after him. She goes to her own room).

SCENE TWO

A fortnight later; night.

Nanna is alone. She fills a cup with milk from the tankard and sits close by the fire supping it. She lifts her head when she hears a delicate tapping at the door. The tapping is repeated when she does not answer immediately.

Slowly Nanna rises and goes to the door. She opens it. Enter Pats.

Pats:	I'm for the past hour at the four sides of the house watching and waiting to know would I see were you alone or was there someone here with you.
Nanna:	I'm alone now, but I won't be for long. Mike will be from the bog shortly. He should be here now, whatever is keeping him.
Pats:	'Tis a good thing you are alone, anyway. *(Looks around)* and that there's no one to hear or see.
Nanna:	There's a great air of trickery about you.
Pats:	I saw the young, Sive, and the other one going the road to town airly in the day.
Nanna:	Gone to buy the wedding clothes they are. Fifty Pounds Dota gave to buy the clothes and the drink for the wedding.
Pats:	'Tis about the wedding I came. Last night we made a plan in the caravan.

Nanna:	What good is a plan now with the wedding tomorrow morning? The poor child is nearly out of her mind these past weeks.
Pats:	At the caravan last night we were boiling a hare, and two of us, when who should arrive but Liam Scuab, that has the notion for Sive. A fine gradhbhar boy he is, and his heart broke for love of the girl. He haven't laid eyes on her this long time.
Nanna:	They keep her in the house all the time. There's always a one to watch her for fear she'd go out.
Pats:	We thought of a plan, the three of us. And the plan is for the girl to steal out of the house tonight. He will be waiting for her at his own place.
Nanna:	They watch her every minute.
Pats:	After she go to bed, who will watch her?
Nanna:	*(Excitedly)*. 'Tis true, and there's a window to the room.
Pats:	She will go in whatever clothes she will be wearing. Whisht ... *(pause)*. Did you hear the sound of a step?
	(Both listen).
Nanna:	'Twas nothing! What else will she do?
Pats:	She will go to the young man's house and they will be married as soon as possible.
Nanna:	'Twill be a great suck-in for all of them!
Pats:	Dota, the farmer, has no business with a young girl. If he have a mind for women let him lie down with his own equals. He have no love for her. 'Tis the flesh of her he do be doting over. The young man have a true heart for her. She have a true heart for him. What more!
Nanna:	*(Giving him a coin)*. God spare you to the roads you travel, Pats, for last night's work.
Pats:	'Twas done willing! God the Master makes His own reward!
Nanna:	Will they marry for sure in the morning?
Pats:	They will marry for sure. *(Takes a letter from his pocket)*. When Sive comes from the town, give her this. There is writing inside that will tell her all. Let no one see you or they will rise to the scent. 'Tis the one chance we have.
Nanna:	*(Takes letter)*. No one will see, I promise you. May God reward you for your goodness.
Pats:	'Tis a small thing to do for my sins, and I have them in a plenty.
Nanna:	It might be the best if you went away now.
Pats:	There's more to go yet. When the woman come from the town I will come again. Carthalawn, my son, will come too. We will sing a song, moryah, and give our blessing to the wedding. They will think that all is well if we pretend to expect the marriage of Dota and the girl.
Nanna:	Go now and God speed you!
	(Suddenly Mike appears in the doorway).
Mike:	I saw you coming, Pats Bocock, and I was watching you around the house. Like a spy you were; peeping and ducking like a spy!
	(Nanna hurriedly conceals letter, noticed by Mike).
Pats:	I have gone through many a place in my travels, but 'tis the first time I was called a spy.
Mike:	*(Entering)*. What were you doing, then, around the house? Looking here and there and walking on your toes!

35

Pats:	Thinking to steal a few eggs I was, but I changed my mind and said to myself that I would ask first before I went stealing.
Mike:	No one would refuse you for an egg in this house.
Pats:	Ah, sure, I know that well, but there is no fun in eating eggs unless they are stolen!
Mike:	*(Suspicious).* You're making up, I'm thinkin'! I don't know what thing brought you, but I'd say 'twas nothing good.
Pats:	I've done you no harm but if I'm not wanted, I'll go.
Mike:	And I've done you no harm and you were always welcome here and you always will. But come straight to the house from the road and there will be a warmer welcome for you. No man likes to have his house watched.
Pats:	God forbid I should make a watch on a man or his house. A man who will spy upon another man or upon another man's woman is a troubled man. Goodnight to the two of ye and God bless.
Mike:	And God bless to you!
	(Exit Pats).
Mike:	What did he want, mother? What was the tinker doing here?
Nanna:	Must a mother answer to her only son? Is there no respect for old people?
Mike:	I have always tried to please you. I never gave lip. It is hard to be a good son and a good husband under the same roof. *(Sits down and leans forward, looking into space).*
Nanna:	We were happy and content here before that woman came into the house. Where is the love you used to have for Sive? Everywhere you went you used to take her with you. You were better than a father to her. Where is the promise you gave to your sister?
Mike:	*(Harried).* Will you not be tormenting me again. Didn't I say to you that a horse can't be guided two roads at once. *(Suspiciously).* And what is it you were hiding from me when I came in? You expect me to be open with you, while you play trickery with the tinker. Tell me what it was you were hiding?
Nanna:	I have nothing to hide from you.
Mike:	There you are now, telling me lies again!
Nanna:	I'll tell you the truth if you'll promise on your word as my son that 'twill be secret.
Mike:	I promise on my word as your son! *(Solemnly).*
Nanna:	*(Withdrawing letter).* 'Tis a letter from Liam Scuab to Sive. There is no harm in it. Only saying good-bye to her in his own way. 'Tis the kind of notion young people have! Little faldals between them.
Mike:	Why was Pats Bocock prowling in the yard?
Nanna:	He was afraid to give the letter to anyone but me. Sure, if your wife or Thomasheen Sean Rua got hold of it, wouldn't they only set fire to it.
Mike:	Are you sure there's nothing more in it?
Nanna:	Wouldn't I tell you if there was?
Mike:	*(Reflectively).* Mmmmmh!
Nanna:	And would I be such a fool as to show it to you if there was anything more in it?
Mike:	That's true, I suppose.
Nanna:	Mike, my son, I know that in your own heart you're against this match. I know you do be thinking your own thoughts about it, about that little wraneen of a man and your sister's child that you love.

36

Mike:	Mother, will you leave me alone! Ye'll see me out of my mind between all of ye.
Nanna:	Give her this letter yourself, Mike.
Mike:	Oh, no!
Nanna:	She will never get it so, because they will be watching for me to leave my room and they would see me giving it to her.
Mike:	I ... I ... I can't, mother! *(Dread sincerity)*.
Nanna:	'Twill be the last bit of comfort or consolation she'll have from this night to her grave.
Mike:	Good God! Why are ye all at me!
Nanna:	If you have a bit of love left in you for Sive and me, you will take this letter and give it to her. What harm will it do? Sure, there's nothing inside in it only a last goodbye and wishing her joy for her wedding.
Mike:	Mother, I would do anything in my power, but ...
Nanna:	Then do this small thing I ask you. No one will know and you will bring joy to your mother's heart and maybe a small bit of joy for Sive.
Mike:	Give me the letter!
Nanna:	*(Handing letter to him)*. God bless you, my son.
Mike:	*(Crosses to the fireplace for his glasses)*. I'm doing wrong by Mena, but it can't do any harm if he's only saying goodbye.
Nanna:	And you won't read it?
Mike:	*(Suddenly)* Why ... why shouldn't I read it?
Nanna:	Ah wouldn't you know yourself the little private things they had between them. If the letter was opened she would only throw it in your face and she'd hate you more for it. Leave the letter sealed. It is a kind of a thing a girl would like to have for a keepsake after she'd be married.
Mike:	*(In a quandary)*. You're very anxious I shouldn't read it.
Nanna:	Did I read it myself? And I have it before you. You made a promise you'd give it. Stick to your promise.
Mike:	*(Irritably)*. I'll stick to my promise.
Nanna:	God will reward you, Mike ... *(The dogs bark)*. You're a good son in your heart.
	(Nanna exits quickly to her room).
	(Mike looks at the letter for a few moments. He places it on the mantelpiece and looks at it for a moment longer. He takes a brush and crosses to sweep around the meal sacks. The door opens and Thomasheen enters, dressed as usual. He gives his usual furtive glances).
Thomasheen:	There was a great housekeeper lost in you. You have the games and the antics of a woman the way you handle the brush.
Mike:	You are in great fettle at the heel of the day!
Thomasheen:	What is the news by you Mike: News! What news would I have, man, that was in the depth of the bog all day, footin' turf?
Thomasheen:	Are they back from town yet?
Mike:	*(Innocently)*. And what would anyone be doing in town?
Thomasheen:	*(Laughs)*. Oh, wisha Mike, will you not be playing Moll the Wag? Who is in town but herself and the girl. Didn't I see Sean Dota giving Mena 50 pounds to buy finery for

37

	tomorrow's wedding.
Mike:	God gave you great eyes.
Thomasheen:	He gave them to the right man. 50 pounds was a great bundle of money for a bit of clothes.
Mike:	*(Defensively).* It was given for Sive's clothes and it will be spent on Sive's clothes.
Thomasheen:	*(Crossing to the fire).* Given for Sive but the two of us know that Mena will have 40 out of the 50 for herself.
Mike:	You're a great mind for putting and taking with sums of money.
Thomasheen:	God gave me that, too. Sure, what harm is it if herself makes a few pounds in the buying of the clothes. Doesn't she deserve it. She worked hard for the wedding, God knows. *(Turns and walks towards window).*

(Mike does not answer. He crosses to the fire. He glances around to see Thomasheen looking out of the window and furtively takes the letter to hide in his pocket. As he is doing so, Thomasheen turns suddenly).

Thomasheen:	Since when did Mike Glavin start putting nothing into his pocket?
Mike:	Well, if your mind is that curious, it was a letter, although it's none of your business or mine but as little.
Thomasheen:	*(Laughs).* Until I have a hundred sovereigns in my breast pocket, I will make business out of everything. Who is the letter for?
Mike:	Sive.
Thomasheen:	Sive, is it? And who is it from?
Mike:	How would I know? Bocock the tinker handed it in, passing the way. I'm keeping it for her.
Thomasheen:	*(Alert and serious. Then, with alarm).* And the letter is for Sive?
Mike:	That's what I told you! Somebody wishing her well, I suppose, on the eve of her wedding.
Thomasheen:	And what will you do with the letter?
Mike:	I will give it to Sive, of course, when she lands from town. What else would I do with it?
Thomasheen:	It comes to me now and again about you!
Mike:	What comes to you?
Thomasheen:	It comes to me that you are the greatest lump of a fool, of an eejit, of a dull amu, in the seven parishes. You shouldn't be trusted with a quenched match. How do you know what is in the letter? Wishing her well, how are you? If you ever get out of the bog and put a few days aside for journeying there is an asylum for lunatics where you could put down a bit of time without doing yourself any harm.
Mike:	*(Frowns)* in misunderstanding). It is only a letter.
Thomasheen:	*(Mimics Mike).* Only a letter!
Mike:	What harm could be in a few words of writing?
Thomasheen:	*(Patiently).* Aaah! My dotey God! What would be in it but thoughts to disturb her young head the night before her marriage. Have you no knowledge of the way a woman do be the night before? Turning and twisting and wondering if she is doing right or wrong. A woman never knows from one minute to the next what way her mind is going to act. 'Tis their affliction. 'Tis the way they are made. You must make up the mind for them. You must whip them up and keep them going, or, like a giddy heifer on the road to the fair,

the next thing you know she'll let a screech out of her, cock her tail up high in the air and break through the first gap in a hedge into some other man's land, and be content there.

Mike: What signifies that?

Thomasheen: Little you know! Open the letter and read out the contents of it.

Mike: It isn't your letter.

Thomasheen: Will you take it out of your pocket and not be playing the gom?

Mike: *(Taking out the letter).* But it is Sive's letter and it is marked 'Private' with a red pencil.

Thomasheen: If it was marked with green, white and yellow and sealed with a Bishop's ring it will have to be opened. Will you not be tormenting me now, and open it.

Mike: *(Yielding).* But, sure, what harm ...?

Thomasheen: *(Assumes a tearful tone, in mockery).* Will you open it or you'll drive me to Gleann na nGealt where your own equals do be.

Mike: *(Pause).* Isn't she getting married tomorrow. Let her have the letter. 'Tis private, look.

(He holds the letter at arm's length. With a swift adroit movement Thomasheen snatches the letter and tears it open. He takes the sheets of folded notepaper from the envelope and opens them. He looks at them and hands them to Mike).

Thomasheen: Read!

Mike: Read yourself!

Thomasheen: I have no time for schoolin' when I was a boy. Read it now an' don't be makin' trouble for yourself.

(Mike takes the letter hesitantly and peruses the first page).

Mike: *(Disgustedly).* You read it! That's Sive's letter.

(Mike hands the letter back to Thomasheen who holds up his hand in rejection).

Thomasheen: *(Embarrassed).* Will you not be mocking. The letter is only like the print of a bird's claw in snow to me. *(Then, firmly).* You read it out or I'll take it the road down to Seamus Donal's.

Mike: *(Resignedly).* All right! All right! I'll read it but it goes against the grain by me.

(Mike takes a pair of spectacles from his breast-pocket and commences to read. His voice is slow, laborious, hardly doing justice to the letter).

Mike: *(Reading).* "My dearest Sive ..."

Thomasheen: Aaah!

Mike: *(Concentrates on letter which presents him with a difficult problem. Reading).* "My dearest Sive, you may remember the last time I spoke to you when I met you coming from school ..."

Thomasheen: Go on! *(He enjoys himself beyond measure).* Go on, let you! Do it say there who 'tis from?

Mike: *(Finds end of letter and reads).* "Yours eternally, Liam."

Thomasheen: Oh, boys! Oh, boys!

Mike: *(Coughs, reads).* "... I have heard from Carthalawn and Pats Bocock, the tinker-poets, that you are getting married to Sean Dota, the farmer ..."

Thomasheen: Would you say now that it was a private letter? *(Triumphantly).* Would you say now that it shouldn't be read? *(Contemptuously).* Go on, man, and read the contents of it.

Mike: ... "Sive, my dearest Sive, I find it impossible to believe that you are marrying this wizened little man of your own accord ... *(reading faster)* ... do you not remember the nights, the starry nights, we spent together in the deep of the bog. There was the quiet and the peace of what we felt for each other. I loved you then, Sive. I love you now ..."

Thomasheen: He did, indeed! Aha! the scoundrel! Breaking up honest homes. *(Waxes violent)*. Has he no love for the law of the land and the voice of the priest?

Mike: Will you hold your tongue and let me finish! *(Worried tone)*. "You are certain to think here that I am beginning to wax poetic ..."

Thomasheen: Wax? *(Loudly)*. He's wax from head to heel! *(Knowingly)*. He will never have a woman the way he is going about it! There is no wax in the ketching of women. There is the ketchin' of a hoult until she is winded. That's the time for words with a woman.

Mike: Do you want me to read the letter or will I leave it?

Thomasheen: Go on! Go on, blast you! You're mad for the word on paper. *(Mike turns over a page and continues, for a moment master of the situation because he can read, also obviously impressed by the sincerity of the letter)*.

Mike: *(Reading)* "... so I have made a decision with regard to you. I believe you are being forced into this marriage against your will. If that is the case and I hope with all my heart that it is, I beg of you Sive, to do as I say. Tonight when they have all gone to bed, steal away quietly and come to my house. I will be waiting there for you. We will drive straight to the city and be married there the first thing. Remember, I will wait for you through the whole night ..."

Thomasheen: Oh, the juice of the roses! Oh, the blood of the grape!

Mike: *(Reading)* "... if you do not come, I will take it that you are content with your choice."

Thomasheen: Oh, the moon and the stars!

Mike: "If this be so, good-bye and God keep you safe. Yours eternally, Liam."

Thomasheen: Ah! They had it well planned! God always finds out a rogue. Trying to steal away the poor innocent girl in the dark of the night.

(Mike folds the letter and places it on the table. He takes off his glasses, and lifts the torn envelope from the ground. It is obvious that the letter has rattled him).

Mike: What will we do?

Thomasheen: I don't know! *(As Mike is preoccupied with his thoughts, Thomasheen takes the letter in the tongs and burns it over the fire)*.

Mike: *(Angrily)*. What are you doing?

(Mike tries to snatch the letter but Thomasheen roughly pushes him away. He drops the letter and envelope to the ground).

Thomasheen: Leave it burn! What she don't know won't trouble her. Our man will have a long wait below. *(He crushes the burning letter under his foot)*.

Mike: The letter was Sive's!

Thomasheen: Will you hold your tongue, you bleddy oinseach! Keep your gob shut. There's the noise of the pony and car on the bohareen. Forget about the letter. You don't know the harm you might cause. When she comes, pretend nothing.

Mike: God direct me, but am I doing right by the girl at all? *(He says this half to himself)*.

Thomasheen: In the honour of God will you be one way or the other, will you? ...Will you? ... *(Raises his voice)*. You're like an oul' hen, dodgin' an dartin', not knowin' what way to turn. Straighten yourself out, man, and be your age for one time in your life.

40

	(Thomasheen goes to the window and looks out).
Thomasheen:	They're in the yard ... they've the car loaded with stuff ... Aha! Cases of porter! The devil knows what!
	(Thomasheen turns to the door and rubs his hands together with great delight. Mena enters the kitchen. She carries a large brown papered parcel under one arm and a smaller parcel under the other).
Mena:	*(Crossly).* 'Tis a wonder one of ye didn't open the door when ye saw me coming with my hands full.
Mike:	Where is Sive?
Mena:	She is coming.
	(Sive enters and stands self-consciously in her new clothes).
Mike:	There's style.
Mena:	Go out to the car and bring in the boxes and don't be standing there with your hands hanging.
	(Without a word, both men go out, Mike in the lead. Sive takes off a pair of new high-heeled shoes which she is wearing and rubs her soles fondly, religiously, with her right hand, balancing with her left hand resting on the table. Slowly she takes off coat and hat. She wears a smart blue frock underneath. She takes coat and hat to the room near the hearth. Mena, the parcels in her hands goes after Sive into the room. Immediately Mike and Thomasheen enter, carrying a crate of stout between them. Mike removes a chair from between the dresser and the door and puts the box in its place. He goes to dresser, finds a bottle-opener and deftly uncaps two bottles, one of which he hands to Thomasheen. He puts the opener in his pocked).
Mike:	Go mheirimid beo!
Thomasheen:	Good luck to us all and bad luck to no one!
	(Both drink heartily from the bottles, lower them, lift them secondly in unison and drain the bottles, which they return to the box. They then hurry out to the yard again. Sive enters the kitchen wearing a pair of low shoes. She sits on a chair near the fire holding her hands in her lap awkwardly.
	Thomasheen and Mike return with a second crate which they put on top of the first. Both look cautiously at Sive and then at each other. Sive does not look up at them.
	Mena arrives into the kitchen).
Mena:	Will ye hurry up, for God's sake, and bring in the other boxes.
	(Both men go out again and Mena places a hand on Sive's shoulder).
Mena:	We will have a bit to eat now. There are sausages and rashers and sweet cake to follow.
Sive:	*(Without looking up).* I'm not hungry. *(Tired and dispirited).* I think I'll go to bed instead. My head is on fire.
Mena:	You haven't put a bit inside of you all day. How do you think you will feel if you don't eat?
Sive:	I don't feel any desire for food. *(Absently).* I would like to lie down.
	(Mike and Thomasheen enter the kitchen again carrying a large tea chest between them).
Mena:	Put it down there! *(They place it aside).*
Mike:	I think I will chance a bottle of stout after that.

Thomasheen: It never did harm!

(*Mena looks with disapproval at him when Mike extracts two bottles from the upper crate. He returns and hands one to Thomasheen, having opened both*).

Mena: (*To Mike, with caution*). Don't you know what that stuff does to you? We'll be having you puking and choking for the rest of the night like a sick cat.

(*Thomasheen and Mike drink from the bottles*).

Mike: 'Tis alright, woman! 'Tis alright!

Thomasheen: Is the stomach delicate with you?

Mike: (*To Sive, in a kind tone*). Will you have a drop of lemonade, Sive, or maybe a suppeen of wine to warm you?

Sive: (*Sighs*). No! I have no mind for it.

Mena: (*Not crossly*). And what will you have? You're not hungry and you're not thirsty. Is there anything you have a mind for?

Sive: (*Shakes her head*). No, nothing!

Mena: I don't know what to say to you.

Sive: (*Rises, slowly, wearily*). I think I'll go to bed now.

Mena: The bed is made and ready for you. Maybe you will feel like something later on.

(*Sive walks slowly to her room. Mena watches her hard-eyed. Exit Sive. Mena goes to dresser and puts three saucers on table*).

Mena: Will you go out and untackle the pony. Do you want the poor animal to die on his feet?

(*Mike finishes his bottle, places it in crate and hurries out closing the door. Mena returns to dresser and puts out three cups on the saucers*).

Thomasheen: Well?

Mena: Well, what?

Thomasheen: Is everything going right with the girl?

Mena: I told you there is no need to worry about that part of it. Mind you collect what is due to us in the morning.

Thomasheen: When the ring is on her finger, I'll handle the money. There is no fear Sean Dota will part with a farthing before his time.

Mena: Oh, you needn't tell me!

Thomasheen: He gave you 50 pounds to buy finery. (*He advances with bottle in hand*).

Mena: It was wanted!

Thomasheen: You could buy out a shop for 50 pounds.

Mena: He gave me the money, me to do what I liked with it. I bought the best, and if there is a shilling or two left over who is better entitled to it than me

Thomasheen: There was a letter from Liam Scuab for Sive!

Mena: What!

Thomasheen: He was for giving it to her. (*He indicates outside where Mike has gone*).

Mena: The fool! Where is the letter now? Where is it?

Thomasheen: Calm yourself, woman! Calm yourself! I took it from him and burned it.

Mena: A good night's work!

Thomasheen: And what way is the old woman?

Mena: I am from the house all day. She never appeared yesterday or the day before.

Thomasheen: Just as well.

> *(The door opens and Mike enters. Immediately he takes a bottle from the crate. Thomasheen drains his quickly and puts it in the crate. He takes the bottle from Mike's hand and hands another from crate to Mike.*
>
> *Leisurely Mike thrusts his hand into his trousers pocket and produces the opener. Thomasheen holds the bottle steady whilst Mike uncaps it. Mike uncaps his own and sits on the sacks. Thomasheen sits upon the tea chest. Both raise the bottles to their mouths and quaff deeply).*

Mena: Ye will have nothing left the way ye're going. Tomorrow is to come yet, take care.

Mike: *(Lifting his bottle to remonstrate).* Only a few oul' bottles of porter.

Thomasheen: *(Who is a joy unto himself).* We will be in the middle of plenty soon!

Mike: There is company, the road up. I saw him far down ...

Mena: *(Much interested).* Who is that?

Mike: Dota! *(Lifts bottle and drinks).*

Thomasheen: Long life!

Mike: Long life to us!

Mena: Sean Dota?

Mike: Sean Dota, the farmer! *(Drinks).*

Mena: Will you go aisy with that! D'you remember the last time you drank porter. D'you remember the state of the room after you. You're like a pet bonham snugglin' and sucklin' for all the good it's doing you. Will you ever come to the age of sense?

Thomasheen: *(Solemnly).* It might be safer to give no drink to what's comin'! If he had a fall on the road and gave over life wouldn't we be in a nice state with the whole country laughing at us in the morning..

Mena: He's in safe keeping here. *(Raises her head and listens).* Hold aisy! He's down on the door!

> *(Thomasheen suddenly comes to his feet and withdraws to the far side of the working table. Delicately he lifts bottle to his lips, and drinks slowly, keeping his eye on the door. There is a timid knock on the door. Mena goes to it and opens door. Sean Dota enters, apologetically and with his customary half-laugh he salutes them).*

Thomasheen: Mind your head, Sean.

Mena: Sean, will you sit up to the fire?

Sean Dota: *(Who is dressed as before, raises a deprecatory hand and laughs apologetically).* No fire for me, thank you. No fire. *(He surveys kitchen, hands behind back).*

Thomasheen: *(Closing the front door).* Soon enough you will have the fire to your side, you diggle, you!

Sean Dota: *(Laughs apologetically).* Ho-ho! the joker! *(He shakes his head).*

Mena: Will you sit down? You must be a bundle of nerves in wait for the morning?

Sean: *(Laughingly).* Oh, wisha, indeed now! I came to see if all was right.

Mike:	Rest yourself Sean! All is right!

Mike: Rest yourself Sean! All is right!

(Sean sits on the chair to the right of the kitchen table).

Mena: Sive is resting in her room.

Sean: The bit of rest is good.

Mike: The weather is holding up fine.

Sean: The rain is threatening this long time. *(Laughs)*. When 'twill fall 'twill fall heavy, I'm thinking. 'Twill be no harm. Won't it give rise to growth.

Thomasheen: True for you.

(Mena goes to dresser and takes out small plates which she distributes about table. She bends to the lower part and takes out a large plate of home-baked bread. The men keep talking).

Mike: There is talk of the milk rising.

Sean: *(Laughs)* No harm indeed to rise it. Great waste going into the feeding of cows. Ye are celebrating, I see.

Mike: So well we might, it being the night it is!

Sean: *(Laughs)*. Oho!

(Mena takes knives and spoons from dresser and puts them on table. She slices the bread).

Mike: Will you take something yourself, Sean?

Sean: *(Laughs)*. Oho! *(He casts a quick glance at the crate of bottles).*

Mike: It never poisoned a man yet.

Sean: *(Laughs)*. Well ... I suppose ...

Mena: *(Turns to Sean, with knife upraised in her hand)*. No man should taste the taste of drink the night before his marriage.

Mike: That's true.

Mena: I will pour out a nice bottle of lemonade for you. Now, Sean.

Sean: Don't mind me! I'll just sit here for myself.

Mena: I'll put a place at the table for you.

(Mena goes to dresser and puts out another cup and saucer on the table. She then takes a jug from the dresser and fills it from the tank, drying the bottom of it with a cloth. She puts the jug on the table).

Mike: *(Raises a hand for silence)*. Whisht yeerselves!

(They all listen attentively, then unmistakably comes the sound of a bodhran in the distance, growing in volume. Thomasheen slips unobtrusively to the fire and puts his back to it, fearfully).

Thomasheen: 'Tis Bocock and his son.

Mike: Come in, let you.

(The tapping of the stick is heard upon the door, in time with the bodhran. Pats and Carthalawn appear in the doorway. Carthalawn is playing and singing).

Carthalawn:	Come now listen while I sing
	To the blessing that I bring
	To the bridegroom and his lovely bride so fair
	May they dwell in wedded joy
	May they ever hear the cry
	Of a new big bouncing baby every year.

Mike: Great work! Great work! Ye're welcome to these parts. Will ye drink porter?

(Mena stands by, arms folded, scowling).

Pats: We will indeed! We saw the boxes coming up the tar-road with the porter-bottles buck-jumping inside in them. I would follow a box of porter to the gates of hell and beyond it if I was dry.

(Mike takes two bottles from the crate, opens them, and hands them to Carthalawn and Pats. He replaces his own empty bottle and opens another for himself).

Pats: That we might never want!

(Pats toasts Mike, Mike quaffs his bottle. Pats and Carthalawn empty their bottles at one swallow. Mike returns to his chair with his bottle).

Mike: Let ye sit down?

Pats: We would sooner stand.

Mike: Ye know all here?

Pats: We do, indeed.

Mike: Ye know Sean Dota, who is for marriage in the morning?

Pats: *(Meaningly).* We know the farmer.

Mike: What is the news from the country?

Pats: There is money making everywhere. The face of the country is changing. The small man with the one cow and the pig and the bit of bog is coming into his own. He is pulling himself up out of the mud and the dirt of the years. He is coming away from the dunghill and the smokey corner. The shopkeeper is losing his stiffness. 'Tis only what I see in my travels. The farmer will be the new lord of the land. What way will he rule? What way will he hould up under the new riches? There will be great changes everywhere. The

servant boy is wearing the collar and tie. The servant girl is painting and powdering and putting silkified stockings on her feet and wearing frilly small clothes under her dress. 'Tis only what I see in my travels. The servant will kick off the traces and take to the high road. Money will be in a-plenty. (He points at Sean Dota). The likes of him will be the new lords of the land. God help the land!

Mena: You're full of dare to insult a dacent respectable man in my house.

Pats: 'Tis only what I see in my travels, a-woman - only what I see in my travels.

Thomasheen: Well, ye can be travelling out of here now. The cheek of ye!

Pats: Carthalawn! Your best! *(He taps with his stick).* Your mighty best!

(Pats taps with his stick again and Carthalawn takes up the time. Then the sounds decrease and Carthalawn sings).

Carthalawn:	*(Singing):* May he screech with awful thirst
	May his brains and eyeballs burst
	That melted amadaun, that big bostoon,
	May the fleas consume his bed
	And the mange eat up his head,
	That black man from the mountain, Seaneen Rua.

Mike:	Great work! Great work! *(He slaps his knee with his hand in glee).*
Sean:	Ho-ho! Ho-ho!
	(Thomasheen fumes with rage. Mena scowls at the tinkers).
Mike:	Ye never lost it! 'Pon my word, ye never lost it!
	(Sean Dota rises).
Sean:	I will be for the road. God knows, I will have an early start in the morning.
Mena:	Will you wait till I call Sive up from the room. She will be dying to see you before you go.
Sean:	*(Changes his mind quickly and sits on the chair again).* By God! I'll wait a minute or two, so!
	(Mena goes into the room by the hearth).
	(Pats sweeps off his hat and holds it in front of Sean).
Pats:	Something to bring luck to you! A handful of silver!
Sean:	How soft you have it! Money for nothing, how are you?
	(Pats retreats dignified to stand in line with his son).
Mike:	You must be getting tired, Sean? I know what is the feeling of a day before marriage.
Pats:	It will be a rest for the poor man to marry.
Sean Dota:	*(Laughs).* A rest?
Pats:	The young girl will be the death of you.
Sean:	How dare you! How dare you, tinker?
Pats:	A squeeze out of a lively young girl would stop your heart, old man. Cathalawn, your best! Your mighty best!
Carthalawn:	*(Sings)* May his hens lay clods and stones May the east wind blight his bones May warts and welts waylay him by the score. Now I swear upon this verse He'll be travelling soon by hearse And we'll never see Sean Dota anymore.
Mena:	*(Re-entering, hysterically).* She's gone! There's a bundle of clothes under the quilt where she should be lying. She's after stealing away on us!
Thomasheen:	*(Seizes her by the arm, roughly).* What are you screeching about? Catch a hould of yourself?
Mena:	She's gone, I tell you! The window of the room is open!
Thomasheen:	Did she take baggage with her?
Mena:	No! ... No! ... Nothing! not even a shoe for her feet.
Thomasheen:	Would she have stolen around to the old woman's room?
	(Mena breaks from his grasp and hurries to Nanna's room to look in).
Thomasheen:	*(Loudly).* Well? Is she there?
Mike:	*(Stands up).* Where could she have gone at this hour of the night, without a shoe or a coat on her?
Pats:	There was something a while ago and we coming up from the cross.

Thomasheen: Out with it! What?

Pats: *(Frowning).* It may be that my eyes would be fooling me but I thought I saw the figure of a girl flashing across the bog near the end of the cutaway where the deep holes do be. I thought it might be a shadow.

Mena: *(Composed again).* And why didn't you say so when you came?

Pats: How was I to know if the sight of my eyes was going or coming? It was only now that you talk about the girl that I think it might have been the girl, Sive.

Thomasheen: You oul' bocock! you oul' dirty twisted bocock! Damn well you knew!

Pats: I did not know, and what is it to me if all the people of the parish ran over the bog in the middle of the night with bare feet.

Mena: What if she fell into a hole ... Oh, my God! *(She shrieks at Mike).* Find her! Find her! ... Hurry yourself!

Mike: I'll get a lantern in the stable ...

(Mena rushes to the room by the fireplace and returns almost immediately with the rubber waders. Mike kicks off his shoes and pulls on the waders).

Thomasheen: I will go with you.

Sean Dota: I will go along with ye.

Mena: Stay, Sean! I will not stay here alone by myself. Stay, somebody. Stay with me. I won't be alone!

(From outside, a frantic voice is heard).

Liam Scuab: Show light! ... Show light! ... Leave open the door ... I am coming over the bog.

(Thomasheen opens the door fully. Mena hurries with the oil lamp to the door. Mike hurries to the door. All exchange frightened glances.

They retreat from the door as Liam draws near. Their faces are horrified as they stand back.

Enter Liam. He is bareheaded and his clothes are wet. His face is ghastly pale. In his arms he carries Sive. Her hair is plastered to her head and her slight body hangs limp in Liam's arms. Liam advances without looking to left or right. At the table he stops.

Pats comes forward and with his stick sweeps the table clean. The ware clatters on the ground breaking the silence. Reverently Liam lays the motionless body on the table. The water drips on to the floor from both Liam and Sive. Liam folds Sive's hands across her breast. Mena replaces the lamp).

Liam: A cloth to dry her hair!

(Mena hands Liam a cloth. Thomasheen edges in to look at the body, then horrified, edges slyly away and exits, looking around him furtively. He is noticed only by Sean Dota who follows him, backing, sneaking, to the door, Sean exits).

Liam: *(Tearfully).* I saw her running across the bog with only the little frock against the cold of the night. She ran like the wind and she letting cries out of her that would rend your heart. *(Filled with sorrow).* I called after her but she would not stop. She took her own life. It was a while before I found her. The poor tormented child.

Mena: Drowned, dead.

(Liam turns suddenly on Mena, blazing with anger).

Liam: *(Cries in anguish).* You killed her! You ... you ... you killed her! You horrible filthy bitch! That the hand of Jesus may strike you dead where you stand. You heartless wretch that hunted the poor little girl to her grave.

47

(Mena retreats, shocked, before him, her hand stupidly covering her mouth).

Liam: *(Shrieks).* Go away! ... Go away! ... You are polluting the pure spirit of the child with your nearness. Go away, witch!

(Liam raises the towel clenched in his fist to strike Mena. Mena hurries away back to her room, Liam begins to dry Sive's hair with the cloth, lovingly and with care).

Liam: The beautiful hair of her! *(He takes her hand).* The lovely silky white of her!

Mike: *(Stupidly, idiotically).* The priest ... we must go for the priest ... she must have the priest ... Holy ground ... she must be buried in holy ground ... the priest ... I must go for the priest ...

(Liam gives Mike a scalding look).

Liam: Go for the priest then! ... Go on! ... Go!

(Mike seizes Liam by the two hands).

Mike: I can't go alone! ... There's no luck in going for a priest alone. You know the old saying ...

(Mike is foolish, babbling now. Liam shakes off Mike's hands violently. He seizes Mike by the hand and drags him to the door).

Liam: Come on! ... I'll lead you past where she was drowned. You'll be on the tar road then. You'll find company.

(They both go out leaving Pats and Carthalawn alone with Sive. After a moment Carthalawn goes forward and touches Sive's face with his hand. His face is sad as he looks at her. After a few seconds Pats taps with his stick and Carthalawn draws away slowly. Both men stand to attention. Then, gently, the stick taps, the knuckles very gently tap the bodhran to slow time. Slow of voice and tenderly Carthalawn sings. Pats looks at him tenderly).

Carthalawn: *(Singing):* Oh, come all good men and true,
A sad tale I'll tell to you
All of a maiden fair, who died this day;
Oh, they drowned lovely Sive,
She would not be a bride
And they laid her for to bury in the clay.

(They turn slowly and march slowly in step through the door, Carthalawn still singing gently).

Carthalawn: *(Singing):* Oh, come all good men and true
A sad tale I'll tell to you
All of a maiden fair, who died this day.
Oh, they murdered lovely Sive,
She would not be a bride,
And they laid her dead, to bury in the clay.

(The singing fades, slowly, slowly, as the light fades in the kitchen.

Nanna, in the faint light comes slowly from her room and goes to where Sive is lying. She bows her head over the dead body and weeps silently.

The singing fades away altogether).

FINAL CURTAIN.

48

NOTES